MW01504177

PURPOSE
WORK
NATION

LEADING ORGANIZATIONS IN SERVICE

OF OUR NATION'S POWERFUL PURPOSE

BRANDON PEELE

Printed in the United States of America
First Printing 2022
First Edition 2022

ISBN: 9798411780376

Midwest Book Review of *Purpose Work Nation*

Business and political leaders who want a more purposeful approach to guiding the United States' renewal will find *Purpose Work Nation* just the ticket.

Brandon Peele outlines past perceptions of business as the leader and driver of the nation's successes and failures, opening with the chapter "Business as Religion, Villain, and Savior," contrasting its image and role in U.S. history.

He considers how traditional images of success often didn't (and don't) consider other ethnicities and their experiences or culture, discussing how, too often, "*...our legacy has been one of dominance, dehumanization and dispossession for profit.*"

After laying the groundwork with a review of the history and socioeconomic development of this nation, Peele explores the myths that shaped an economy built on genocide and slavery and its dissonance with the nation's purpose: "*Knowing the truth about our history would not bother us if we took pride in being a bunch of shifty eagles. These truths only bother us because deep down we know we are better than the murdering, thieving, raping, and enslaving of our ancestors. If we didn't hold ourselves to a higher standard, if we didn't have a noble national purpose, reading this would produce no resistance, no knot in the pit of our stomachs.*"

Peele's concept of "bison ethics" suggests a different approach to not just business, but the people who drive its culture. This opens in the second chapter and receives further development as the book moves through systems failures, issues of racial and social justice, the unspoken assumptions in hiring and training, and how relationships may be guided by the ethics of the nation's National Mammal, the bison, as a source of strength.

His focus on best practices and real-world applications creates a new culture and paradigm for success that moves from business to social and political circles: "*To do this, we must think holistically and get at the source of what people need to flourish: a balanced work-load, living wages, flexibility, meaning, connection, care, and believing they matter and are a part of something that matters. The bison way is one of relationships versus the eagle's outputs, of covenants versus the eagle's contracts. It is about establishing our personal covenant with our unique purpose, and with each other around a shared mission. It is the way of nurturing a healthy culture where each of us can activate and fulfill our purpose on the job, and enjoy rich connections with each other.*"

The result is a powerful survey of business and human affairs that links diversity to strength and eschews the predatory, inhumane approaches of the "eagle" in favor of the "bison way" which confronts white supremacy and positions the workplace as the starting place to effect real social and political change: "*The workplace is where we congregate to serve and empower others, to activate our unique purpose, fulfill our potential, nurture community, and achieve our mission. We bring the spirit of the bison home with us and let it guide our family and civic life. In so doing, we activate the purpose of this nation, repair the damage from our nation's misspent youth, and achieve redemption.*"

Readers may initially be drawn by the book's promise of keys to better leadership, but they'll find its wider-ranging approach to building a better culture ripples into society with lasting and positive impacts on human rights that lead to a better quality of life for all.

Idealistic? Yes. Achievable? Absolutely.

No business collection should be without *Purpose Work Nation*, but it's just as highly recommended for libraries strong in social and political issues, civil rights, and American civics.

Diane Donovan, Senior Reviewer, Midwest Book Review

Praise for *Purpose Work Nation*

"Businesses have an outsized role and a fiduciary responsibility to solve the climate crisis. They have a similar role and responsibility to create thriving workplaces. People need to feel safe, valued and a sense of belonging. They need to bring their authentic, purposeful self to work and be fulfilled by their impact and relationships. *Purpose Work Nation* provides leaders with a scalable, evidence-based approach to empower individuals, teams and communities to thrive."

Jeffrey Stier, America's lead: Strategic Purpose + Vision Realized, EY

"In *Purpose Work Nation*, Brandon tackles complicated interwoven topics of race, privilege, business, and governance with particular focus on the U.S., and provides us with some guideposts for progressing with purpose in those four lanes. Brandon is one of the great thinkers of our time, and his story is testament to what can happen when hard work, focus, and brilliance is applied to producing and sharing the gift of purpose with the world. Don't waste one more moment of your existence on this planet not being exposed to his generous, thoughtful, open-minded, action-oriented perspectives."

Gabrielle Blocher, GM, CelerPurus

"Brandon is persuasive and persistent in his quest to make our society better–and he wants to enlist all of us in helping develop a more perfect union. He nudges us beyond the soundbites, the talking points coming from people on both sides who benefit from division, in favor of more thoughtful–and more difficult–exploration. His argument that business has a massive role to play in making change happen resonates strongly with me as someone focused on creativity in the business world. But in the end, businesses are collections of individuals, and so exploring some of the processes and trainings that can engage people where they are, across the spectrum of business roles and hierarchies, might actually be the only way to help this society realize its potential and effectuate change. For that reason, I hope this book is read widely."

Alan Iny, Global Leader, Creativity and Scenarios, Boston Consulting Group

"This is a clarion call for business leaders to put their power, privilege and platforms in service of rehumanizing our society, restoring our republic and regenerating our planet. Not through their own heroic visions, but by humbly co-creating cultures of purpose and belonging through which all people flourish, business thrives, and the dream of 'E Pluribus Unum' becomes a reality. Brandon offers concrete, practical actions that are grounded in organizational research, put into historical context, and enlivened with stories from his own purposeful journey."

Lara Lee, Independent Director WD-40, Marrone Bio Innovations, The Sill

"Eye-opening, direct hits on the many ways we've purloined the right of human flourishing from so many, and the purpose-based solutions for change. Like the bison, Brandon Peele charges directly into the storm, armed with powerful experiences and the latest scientific research. It's a transforming work."

Vic Strecher, PhD, CEO Kumanu, Author of *Life on Purpose*

"*Purpose Work Nation* offers leaders a pathway to activate their teams and free them from mistrust and divisiveness. This book is research-backed, elegant and as American as apple pie. Read it to bring out the most productive and inspired work across the full diversity of your workforce. Given our mighty struggle to achieve social justice, *Purpose Work Nation* presents what is possibly today's most vital lesson for leaders."

Bea Boccalandro, President, Veraworks, Author of *Do Good at Work: How Simple Acts of Social Purpose Drive Success and Wellbeing*

"I've always believed in the power of business to create a flourishing planet. Prior to 2020, not many other CEOs agreed with me. Thankfully, they've caught up quickly. Especially as our nation gives way to chaos and division, business leaders are embracing their leadership legacy by investing in people and caring for their communities and planet.

"*Purpose Work Nation* is a guidebook for how to do that effectively and sustainably. I found Brandon's premise–that business is the only sector that can fulfill our nation's purpose–to be both sobering and inspiring. Rich with research and examples, this book is a must-read for every executive who wants to lead effectively in these uncertain times."

Chip Conley, Founder of Joie de Vivre Hospitality and Modern Elder Academy, Author of *Wisdom @Work*

"*Purpose Work Nation* offers a provocative argument for transformational change that is sure to challenge most American workplaces. After making a compelling case for why business is perfectly positioned to tackle society's most daunting challenges, Brandon shares his inspiring vision of a more diverse, unified, humanistic, and thriving workplace. Through heartfelt storytelling about his own journey about what it means to succeed and thrive in the world of business, Brandon role models the ample courage, vulnerability, and humility required for leaders to take a hard look at the current state of the workplace and to consider how they can effect change. Additionally, the research linking purpose and connection to mental, emotional, and physical well-being make Brandon's recommendations a terrific addition to any workplace well-being strategy. While well-grounded in research, the book is also highly practical. A terrific read to inspire enlivened conversations about your organization's mission and path towards a flourishing world."

Jessica Grossmeier, PhD, MPH – Workplace well-being researcher, CEO, Grossmeier Consulting

"Most of the challenges in the world, from climate change to inequality, can be connected back to companies as the root cause. As Brandon writes, it is imperative that these same companies redirect their resources and creativity to solving them. Brandon outlines how companies can lead with purpose inside and outside their organizations–starting by awakening the purpose of all their employees."

Aaron Hurst, CEO of Imperative, Author of *The Purpose Economy*

"If we're going to have organizations and a society where people can be authentically human, belong, and make a positive contribution and impact, we have to be willing to get uncomfortable and look at the hard truths that have gotten us to this point so we can pave a better path forward. And we can't wait any longer. Brandon eloquently paints the picture to help foster understanding of where we've been, how businesses can be a source of healing and practical ways we can activate purpose and belonging to create a better country for us all. This is a must-read for anyone wanting to have more human, connected workplaces!"

Rosie Ward, PhD, CEO, Salveo Partners and co-author of *Rehumanizing the Workplace*

"Brandon Peele makes a strong case that bottom-up culture building is of greater importance than top-down strategy. With the bison metaphor, he reminds the reader that major culture shifts can only happen when people reimagine their deeply ingrained symbols and narratives. By telling engaging personal stories supported with groundbreaking research, Brandon provides a clear call to action for leaders to activate cultures of purpose and belonging."

Kursat Ozenc, PhD, VP of Design, New Business Ventures Lab, J.P. Morgan Chase & Co., Lecturer, Stanford's d.school

"I wholeheartedly love this book. And I so honor this man who wrote it. Part of the inspiration of this book is that Brandon Peele is an Ivy-educated white guy who reckons with the systemic privileges that have benefited him and hurt others. He doesn't sugarcoat our past and present, and shines a light on the path forward for everyone to flourish and our troubled nation to heal its original sins.

"But this is not a blaming scapegoating book. After Brandon details with great rigor and historical accuracy how America came to its current disjointed, broken and undemocratic state, he guides the reader to explore how our nation's mythology and narrative undermine the values that were inherent in its formation. But rather than just the individualistic approach to becoming more whole and humane, inclusive and diverse, developed and purposeful, Brandon fervently argues that business is the core institution that should be shaping the future soul of our nation. His recommendation for bringing purpose and belonging into workplace culture and systems is a paradoxical and evolutionary shift in how we can put ourselves back together again as a nation.

"This book is a must-read for any business leader who desires to create a place where people can become better humans by going to work."

Holly Woods PhD, Founder of Emergence Institute, Author of *The Golden Thread: Where to Find Purpose in the Stages of Your Life*

"Brandon consistently and creatively demonstrates just how crucial creating diverse, equitable, inclusive, and purpose-driven workplace environments can lead teams to more powerful outcomes and a more sustainable community. One can only appreciate a book with such groundbreaking research and actionable tactics to help leaders become more inclusive and inspiring to their teams and keep moving the U.S. forward."

B. Maurice Ward, DEIB Leader, PEMCO Mutual Insurance

"Based on his research and consulting, Brandon walks us through the frameworks that historical workplace cultures have held and shows us where they are in stark contrast to what organizations need to build a business that benefits both people and profit. In his writing, Brandon also takes us beyond the philosophical, presenting tactical drivers organizations that are the foundation of inclusion and can be implemented immediately to allow all employees to better thrive."

Emily Goodson, CEO, CultureSmart

"*Purpose Work Nation* is the call-to-action that we need! It helps us understand the history of our current issues and a path forward to fix them. I recommend it to anyone leading a team or organization. Let's be Bison."

Eric Winters, Co-Founder of Heylo and former Principal at Google

"I hope everyone reads and embraces this important book. Brandon is a purpose-driven leader who will not rest until the honest conversations have been had. His honest voice opens the eyes, minds and hearts to right the wrongs of so many before us."

Fran Biderman-Gross, Founder of Advantages, NYC, Author *How to Lead a Values-Based Professional Services Firm*

"A unique, engaging, and disrupting perspective on the intersection of work, culture, belonging, and purpose."

Zach Mercurio, PhD, author of *The Invisible Leader: Transform Your Life, Work, and Organization with the Power of Authentic Purpose*

"*Purpose Work Nation* is for leaders looking to make a powerful impact on their organization and on their nation. Brandon shows us how creating truly diverse, inclusive, purpose-driven workplaces helps our teams and our country flourish. The book is full of groundbreaking research and actionable tactics to help leaders leave a meaningful and lasting legacy."

Suzanne Clausen, Director of Client Services, CuraLink Healthcare

"*Purpose Work Nation* lays out a bold vision for the workplace, our economy, and our country. Filled with captivating personal stories, this book makes the irrefutable case for purpose and belonging in today's remote work world. This is the blueprint for employee retention and happiness that I have been looking for."

Tom Drugan, Vice President, Operations, SlideUX

"It is so hard not to drown in despair with the weight of the social, economic, and environmental issues of our time. I am in awe of anyone with the courage to look into the traumas we face and articulate a solution. *Purpose Work Nation* galvanizes change through synthesis of multidimensional insights that arrive at a coherent vision to move humanity forward. This book is part autobiography of a man who has dedicated his life to personal development, part critical deconstruction of popular history and culture, and part guidebook for the next generation of leaders.

"*Purpose Work Nation* is a much-needed wake up call. It bridges worlds, combining research references alongside poetic metaphors. It will break your heart and build you back stronger if you allow yourself to be guided by the process of examination outlined in these pages."

Arezou Ghane, **PhD**, Founder, Auteur Health and Wellness

"Let's be real. From a rapidly changing climate that threatens our very existence, to the COVID pandemic, to a fragile democracy that is crumbling from within like no time since the Civil War, to growing attempts to reinstall Jim Crow, to economic disparity that continues to widen unabated, our country is in a heap of trouble.

"In *Purpose Work Nation*, Brandon Peele lays out in exquisitely referenced detail just exactly how we got where we are. It isn't pretty and sure as hell not what most of us were taught in school. In fact, to right our dangerously listing ship, he suggests we will likely have to 'unlearn everything about U.S. history.'

"But all hope is not lost! Peele then proceeds to propose a solution that involves working through the private sector to help organizations provide opportunities for their employees to embrace their purpose and create the missing authentic connections that Dr. Martin Luther King, Jr. identified as the two key drivers of 'beloved communities.'

"This book is a soulful guide for caring leaders who want to make a difference, not just for their employees, but for their customers, their communities and for the whole of humanity. Peele explores in detail how this can be accomplished and provides extensive data to demonstrate how it actually can and does work.

"If you read only one business book this year, this is the one you want to choose, precisely because it is not primarily about business, but about creating a different and better humanity—one that, paraphrasing Dr. King, bends the moral arc of the universe toward justice."

Jon Robison, PhD, Founding Partner, Salveo Partners

"For many including myself, recent events have caused an enormous sense of dislocation and an urgent query into who we are, what we stand for, and where we are going. Through refreshing honesty about privilege and racial justice and meticulous research across multiple domains of knowledge, Brandon Peele's new book is the truth-telling and inspiration needed to start the nation towards healing and a new level of greatness."

Mary Abad, Executive Director, J.P. Morgan Healthcare Banking

"In his new book, *Purpose Work Nation*, Brandon Peele is asking us to resist recent trends that are diminishing our nation's 'deep calling for equality, justice and liberty' as expressed in our founding documents. Brandon shows us how early values of individualism and independence taken to the extreme have shaped a corporate culture that produced extraordinary wealth for some but at great cost to our nation.

Backed by hard data, he points out that, while such a culture may provide short-term benefits for a few, it cannot deliver a sustainable future that will fulfill our nation's commitment to all its citizens.

"Brandon describes this challenge by using two of our national symbols to represent two different paths we can follow: the path we have been on so far or a new one. Our current path, grounded in the primacy of the individual, is embodied in our national bird, the bald eagle, a solitary and opportunistic hunter and scavenger. A more noble and sustainable path would be oriented towards the welfare of the society as a whole as embodied in our national mammal, the bison, a courageous, social animal that protects the herd. His analogy is a powerful one.

"Pursuing this second path will require a cultural transformation, which according to Brandon has already started in the business world with demonstrable results. He proposes as a first step that each of us discover and activate our purpose at work. Following that, he offers some new approaches to instill the more inclusive values and behaviors of the bison to facilitate more meaningful stakeholder engagement.

"Brandon argues that corporate America is the place to start shifting values and beliefs from a more self-directed and self-serving orientation to one that is more outward-serving in the fulfillment of the organization's purpose; that is, to 'the Bison way.' Business has always been at the forefront of change in America. Brandon sees business again taking a leadership role in getting us back on track to fulfill our national purpose.

"Brandon's book gives me hope that corporate America can be the impetus to move our country and the world beyond our earlier survival instincts to one of inclusion and cooperation. Reading this book has inspired me and hopefully will inspire you to keep up the good fight."

Paul Ratoff, President, Foundation for Purposeful Organizations, Author of *Thriving in a Stakeholder World*

"Many people today bemoan the ugly divisions of American society, but Brandon Peele is one of the few to not just point out the problems loud and clear but to also offer solutions. In *Purpose Work Nation,* Peele points to businesses as the answer, IF they embody and ensure two human experiences: purpose and belonging. Brandon offers leaders tools and insights for how to cultivate purpose and belonging for everyone, which can, as we say, 'make work and the world more human.'"

Renée Smith, Founder and CEO of A Human Workplace

Table of Contents

Gratitude & Acknowledgment

I want to thank the original caretakers of the land upon which I wrote this book, the Kumeyaay Nation. I thank my friends and colleagues who poured their hearts and minds into this book. I'm of the firm conviction that ideas do not arise in a vacuum nor can they be attributed to any single person. They arise in dialogue, through the generous reflection, sharing and dissent of well-meaning people. As such, everything in this book is a result of the thousands of hours of conversations I've had with people who are smarter and better informed than I.

As the possibility of this book emerged, I sent a chapter a week to over 30 experts from fields such as psychology, leadership development, government, organizational development, wellness, diversity, equity and inclusion (DEI), economics, human development, education, history, healthcare, religion, politics, law, facilitation, sustainability, racial justice, manufacturing, corporate social responsibility, technology, and peace and reconciliation. I thank all of you for listening, reflecting, and responding. Special thanks to Susan Lucci, Bea Boccalandro, Bobby Bakshi, Anamaria Aristizabal, Jessica Grossmeier, Paul Ratoff, Robin Athey, Suzanne Clausen, Tim Ash, Stephanie Staidle, Ezra Bookman, and Lara Lee for rolling up their sleeves and beating the nonsense out of this work, line by line.

I also want to thank my friends, mentors, and communities that nurtured my personal and professional growth during the writing of this book. Special thanks to Lara Lee, Bobby Bakshi, Susan Lucci, Aaron Hurst, Maurice Ward, Dena Wiggins, Scott Crosby, Jeff Stier, Stephan Mackenzie, Charles Vogl, Jean-Michel Lauregans, Pat Sandone, Paul Minifee, Eric Zimmerman, Robin Athey, Michael Tertes, Sam Clayton, Govinda Clayton, Matt Stillman, Ted Frelke, Andy Swindler, and the Showing Up for Racial Justice (SURJ), Global Purpose Leaders, ManKind Project, ListenFirst, Google Vitality Lab, and Business For Good communities.

I want to thank Zach Mercurio and Shavon Lindley who allowed me to repurpose portions of "The Purpose and Profits Roadmap" paper we published together in 2019, and the numerous participants in Unity Lab programs who generously offered their feedback to make our programs more scalable and effective. I thank my Unity Lab team for their shared commitment to a more purposeful, just, equitable and compassionate nation, and the hundreds of actions they take each day to make it so. No one deserves more credit than my co-founder, Heidi Holliday.

Last and most, I thank my partner, Stephanie Staidle, for her love, care, and stand for this book and my work in general. My mind and heart have a hard time turning off from my purpose / work and she's been incredibly understanding of my heartache and sleeplessness. I'm grateful for her personal and professional development, as it is a source of inspiration for me, and makes it easy for me to clean up my careless mistakes and broken agreements. Her vision for our home has made it an incredible place to write, live, eat, love, rest, and rejoice. I thank her for allowing me to have the nice room for my office, which has allowed me—at considerable inconvenience to her—to write this book and engage in the hundreds of conversations with leaders, experts, and practitioners who shaped the ideas herein.

Author's Notes

Author's Note #1: Why I wrote this book

In February of 2012, I completed my initial purpose discovery journey, left my career in Silicon Valley, and began to live a markedly different life: one driven and enchanted by my purpose (def. "purpose", a transcendent identity beyond the concerns of self and family that includes many aspects such as one's vision for the world, mission, craft, and most cherished values). In the years since, understanding my purpose has led me to write books, guide others on their purpose journeys, help build a global community[1] of purpose practitioners, travel internationally giving keynotes, and deliver purpose programs for organizations like LinkedIn, Stanford, and the United States Marine Corps. I felt like I was living proof of the power of purpose. I had romance, impact, success, and a deep sense of fulfillment.

In spite of all this, a persistent unanswered question has remained in my heart: Where is home? I thought my soul should have that answer. I have been in regular dialogue with my soul about how to live and how to serve, and it is typically generous with guidance. But on this question, it was curiously quiet. And as a result, I felt unsettled, never fully at home or at peace.

At the end of 2012, I had just moved to Berkeley, California, a town where I knew virtually no one, and so the question loomed even larger. Where is my soil? Who are my people? I was from Illinois and had lived in Chicago, New York, Los Angeles, and San Francisco—but none of these places felt like home. And here I was again, starting over in a new town, feeling unrooted and disconnected.

In retrospect, I was encountering the collective aspects of purpose. Purpose isn't just about me and my gifts and you and your gifts, but it also shows up in how I relate to my family, my community, and my soil. Soul and soil share an etymological root in the way human, humane, and humus do, and natal, nation, and nature do. To be human is to be ensouled, born of the earth, of the humus, to belong to the living soil. And yet, I was a human without soil–an air plant of sorts. Somehow I miraculously pulled in nutrients from the air and sun, but I was alone and longing for the nutrition that only the sense of a shared history and belonging can provide.

To inhabit one's soul or one's purpose is to inhabit one's place on the planet and one's role in community, society, and the economy. In the way other species inhabit an ecological niche, thriving in certain climates and altitudes and perishing in others, humans also have conditions necessary for thriving. In this way, to be a human and not feel at home is disturbing and unsettling. Indigenous tribes, such as the Māori and Diné (Navajo), bury their placenta ceremonially to mark this sacred connection. There are people in Mexico whose phrase for "Where are you from?" translates to "Where is your placenta buried?" The Welsh also offer a word that illuminated the uneasiness I felt in not feeling at home: *hiraeth*, a spiritual longing tinged with soulful grief, an unspecified homesickness, a nostalgia for ancient times and places to which we can never return. Perhaps these are times and places that never were[2].

4

In retrospect, my homesickness was for true belonging, a sense that everyone in my community has dignity, that our unique gifts matter and are celebrated. This was something that my Midwestern upbringing never fully delivered. Growing up white in the suburbs, I had what many might describe as a rich community with family, nature, sports, and school. However, it felt bland and simulated, like everyone was pretending to be happy, like they made it, and this was the best of all possible worlds. Something really important was missing, but I couldn't name it then.

At first, I tried to distract myself from the question of home with my work, dating, hiking, and festivals. I thought I would eventually learn to love living in the Bay Area and believed it would be where I would put down roots and build a community where I truly belonged.

In 2016, Stephanie—my then girlfriend and now wife—and I received some upsetting news: our friends were leaving the Bay. They had little ones and elected to move closer to nature and family. As the majority of our work could be done virtually and a good portion of our community had flown the coop, we found ourselves asking the question together, "Where is home?"

We wanted a place where we could put down roots. We wanted a place where Steph could be warm and surf. We wanted a place that felt real, connected, permanent, and less of a bubble of inequality, disconnection, and transience. We considered the Southeast, Southern California, Spain, and Central America.

When I sat with the option of leaving the United States, I just couldn't picture myself doing it. For all of our nation's problems—and as much as I like sangria in a Spanish plaza and fish tacos on a Baja beach—I couldn't leave. There is something of my soul in this soil: Midwestern lakes, corn festivals, street fairs, baseball, barbecue, the blues, Jeeps, Yosemite, and the Grand Canyon. Each has claimed a piece of my soul.

This much I knew. However, it seemed like at least once a week, I learned something about how my home was falling apart. As it turns out, most of our national family is struggling:

- 97% of us live unhealthy lifestyles[3]
- 84% of us are experiencing higher levels of stress during the pandemic[4]
- 61% of us are lonely[5]
- 50% of us are disengaged or actively oppose our employer[6]
- 49% of us do not make a living wage[7]

And it's even worse for people of color (e.g., Black families have $.01 of wealth for every dollar a white family has[8]).

And we're not just sad, lonely, and broke, but increasingly finding ourselves at odds with each other. We have tensions between conservatives and liberals, Boomers and Millenials, white and BIPOC folks (Black, Indigenous, and People of Color), LGBTQIA+ (Lesbian, Gay, Bisexual, Trans, Questioning, Intersexual, Asexual) and cis-gendered heterosexuals, employees and employers, rural and urban folks. The list goes on and on, and points to a clear lack of integrity. Our country's purpose ("all [people] are created equal," *E Pluribus Unum,*" "Life, Liberty, and the Pursuit of Happiness," and "to form a more perfect union") is increasingly not the reality for the people who call this place home. We are not free, equal, healthy, happy, or connected. And we're pissed. One in three of us believe violence may be necessary to achieve our political goals[9]. Beyond being pissed about our politics and differences, we're pissed at the system. We're pissed at the lie.

We were all sold the lie, the so-called "American Dream": that in the United States, with hard work, anyone can carve out a middle class life with comfort, security, and belonging. With income mobility at historic lows[10], each day more of us are waking up to the fact that even if we become wealthy, it typically means more rooms and higher fences, rather than longer tables, deeper connection and greater fulfillment.

In light of this, how could I leave? How could I jump ship? Our shared purpose means something to me–and it enrages me that we aren't living it, when I know it's possible. I knew I wouldn't be able to live with myself if I jumped ship. So we decided to stay, and also to experiment with living in a new part of California.

After we married in the summer of 2018, we moved to San Diego, a diverse, but segregated, second-tier, purple city (about equal parts conservatives and liberals). Steph could be warm and close to the beach, and we'd have our chance of building a life and community in a place with unspeakable natural beauty and rich diversity.

We moved to a working class neighborhood near the ocean, enjoyed the beach, margaritas, hiking, and burritos. As I started to connect with my neighbors, I saw good people working their butts off just about every damn minute of the week. One neighbor drove a cab at all hours and struggled to fit in an hour or two a week to kick the soccer ball around with his sons in the alley. Another couple, working as a landscaper and a hairstylist, fled for more house and cheaper rent in the Midwest after they had a child. Another had worked at Home Depot for 5 years and made $12/hour. When interviewing cleaning services, I asked how much the cleaners made. Rarely was it higher than $15/hour. I talked with unhomed folks, many who are veterans, many with mental illness and addictions to meth or fentanyl; they wanted to work, but had trouble keeping a job.

My heart broke. Almost everyone was living hand to mouth. The living wage required to support a family of 4 was $40/hour[11], yet few jobs paid more than $15/hour. This meant most households had extended families living together and multiple incomes. For those who weren't part of a solid family, there was the street. With plenty of cheap crack, meth, fentanyl, and oxycontin, and warm weather, San Diego was brimming with folks who had opted out of the struggle / subsistence wage cycle.

Although we certainly had plenty of inequality and poverty in the Bay, it hit me differently in San Diego. Perhaps I had become more open to our nation's pain. Perhaps taking in a new city allowed me to see more deeply what was actually going on. It's hard to say, but the effect was shame and betrayal. Each struggling parent and street kid felt to me like a personal failure.

San Diego gave me a unique view into our hourglass-shaped economy[12], with my San Francisco and New York friends making $200k+/year and posting photos of vacations in Vail and Bali—and my San Diego community scraping by and barbecuing in the park on their one day off.

How could I call myself a citizen and be ok with this? I certainly couldn't ignore it. So I let it in. Throughout 2019, our collective suffering began to teach me. It showed me how the vast majority of us (even the wealthy ones) were living lives of quiet desperation. It showed me that I was not alone in feeling betrayed by our nation's promise.

As 2020 began, I thought I was through the worst of my heartbreak. After all, I was working with great clients building cultures of belonging and purpose. I loved working with my colleagues, giving keynotes, and mixing it up at conferences, karaoke bars, street fairs, and festivals. Steph and I moved to an awesome home in a diverse and walkable neighborhood and started building community.

Ha! Enter COVID-19. Like many folks, we masked up, sequestered, and helped keep our local businesses alive. With in-person outlets closed down, all of my attention poured into our nation's crisis of soul. For me—and I reckon, for many of you—early 2020 was a cascade of soul-piercing heartbreaks. A chaotic pandemic response and our political dysfunction revealed how much hatred was in our house. We were falling apart. My family and friends either avoided the topic of politics or avoided each other. When we did engage, we talked past each other, each inhabiting wildly different worlds, each with different facts, beliefs, conclusions, and visions for the path forward. As if that wasn't enough...

On Tuesday, May 26, 2020, I watched the last 8 minutes and 46 seconds of George Floyd's life. I spent the next couple of days horizontal on the couch in disbelief. It felt like 1995, the year my brother, Carson, died in a car accident. I remember asking myself multiple times a day *Did that really just happen? Is he really gone? Is this real? Am I awake?*

George's death hit me in a similar fashion. *Did I just witness a white man calmly kill a Black man? When a grown man calls out for his dead mother, does that not signal something is wrong? Did his body going limp not suggest he should stop? Did seeing him evacuate his bowels not signal a change to the restraint approach?*

Derek Chauvin's facial expression is stamped on my heart. When we lived in the Bay Area, my wife and I were frequent protesters, well-read about our nation's original sins (genocide and slavery), our ongoing apartheid, and the mechanics of systemic racism[13]. We had engaged in inclusion and diversity trainings. So we knew that this murder wasn't a one-off, but on a long list of unarmed BIPOC people murdered by police (including Trayvon Martin, Eric Garner, Michael Brown, Ahmaud Arbery, and Breonna Taylor).

What was new to me was the look on Derek's face: its unflinching, steady commitment to murder. His face is white and middle-aged, just like mine. It is the face of a man who likely believed he was serving the common good, just like me.

How many times had I hardened my heart and turned away from the suffering of my Black, Hispanic, Indigenous, and Asian friends? How many times did I walk past an unhomed person without acknowledging them or offering help?

How many times did I tolerate racism, sexism, and homophobia? How many times did I join in by telling jokes and poking fun? How many times did I let the love drain from my face, while I justified the suffering of others as natural, normal, and just the way things are?

And then it hit me. Now I know why I don't feel at home in the U.S. and why I can't live in another country: the fulfillment of our purpose has become *my* responsibility. I wasn't elected by anyone, but summoned from within. I just can't take the blue pill, put blinders on, and try to live a cloistered life of comfort, whether in Illinois or New York or California. I can't feel at home or at peace when dehumanization is happening in any room in *my* house. I can't feel at home in a nation with so much unacknowledged and unhealed trauma. I can't feel at home in a place that calls us to kill, oppress, exploit, rape—and then forget any of it happened, and that it continues to happen! I can't fully feel at home until we activate our purpose, heal our wounds and prevent further harm.

Author's Note #2: Choosing Citizenship

I began to realize that my citizenship wasn't just a legal and geographical matter; it is a choice. It's not just saying this is where I live, pay taxes, and observe the laws, but saying that *we* believe in *certain* ideas here, and that it is my choice to either ignore them, do as I please, and try to avoid the consequences, or claim them as my own and defend them. For too long, I chose the former. I can no longer do this.

We are a nation of ideas, rights, and laws constituted by the world's peoples, not a singular people nor faith group. Embedded in our founding documents is a framework for cooperation—a set of principles by which a country of immense beauty, wealth, diversity, and imagination may find guidance and refuge. It is important to note that our nation's ideas were originally envisioned to serve only white, male landowners. However, these ideas were so powerful that they extended beyond the original intentions of our founders. Because of the power of these ideas, we united around and fought for them—sometimes surrendering our lives—to ensure our Constitution expanded to include everyone who calls this land home.

A nation's purpose isn't complete upon utterance. It breathes and has a dynamic life of its own. It requires tending and consecration, asking us to continually make it more real and enduring. It must be ministered, shaped into form, function, and experience. It has to be seen, felt, and measured. If we are to live it, to call ourselves citizens, we must also atone for our failure to consecrate our purpose, heal the impacts of this negligence, and ensure our purpose becomes real for all citizens. This consecration also implies that we keep asking questions of our purpose to uncover new ways of conducting ourselves as a society, government, and economy to fulfill upon it.

The purpose of the United States of America has four key parts:

1. Equality for all,
2. Unity in our diversity,
3. Flourishing for all, and
4. Work tirelessly to ensure that equality, unity, and flourishing expand over time.

To effectuate this purpose in these times of unprecedented crisis and opportunity, we need new language to capture the fullness of its power. For example:

"All [people] are created equal" - We hold this truth to be self-evident, that all people here belong, have dignity, rights, and a clear path to fulfill their potential regardless of their gender, skin color, sexuality, what they look like, how able they are, what they do, how much money they make, how they worship or love, or who their daddy is.

"*E Pluribus Unum*" (**from many, one**) - We perform the sacred task of activating unity in this diverse nation; to continually transform *pluribus* into *unum*; not to be a bland, soulless *Truman Show*, nor a melting pot, nor a mixed salad, but a weave, a diverse tapestry of belonging and celebration, where our open hearts value and love every life, contribution, and culture; to celebrate this diversity as we bind ourselves together: "...indivisible, with liberty and justice for all." *For all.*

"Life, Liberty, and the Pursuit of Happiness" - We build institutions to ensure everyone has ready and affordable access to healthy food, clean soil, air, and water; healthcare, education, and housing (life); to ensure each of us is free and liberated from the constraints of systemic oppression, limiting circumstances and beliefs (liberty); to ensure each of us is fulfilled by discovering and activating our purpose in our career and life and belonging to a powerful community (the pursuit of happiness).

"To form a more perfect union" - We fight like hell to ensure that freedom, equality, prosperity, and unity are available to more and more of us, and in ever-greater amounts, so long as we live.

That's the heart of this book. This book is the declaration: "Not in our house." We do not have the right to call ourselves citizens, much less leaders, if we are not actively consecrating our purpose by bringing healing, liberty, and flourishing to *all* of us.

Author's Note #3: Who this Book is For

This book is for leaders who are moved to do life, career, and leadership differently following the murders of Trayvon Martin, Ahmaud Arbery, Breonna Taylor, and George Floyd. This book is for leaders who were stirred by *Don't Look Up, 12 Years a Slave, Handmaid's Tale,* or *Black Mirror.* This book is for leaders who know that in order to have the impact they want to have tomorrow, they must continue to summon new capacities of leadership.

This book is for the damn-giving, evolutionary leader who knows that leadership is, by definition, uncomfortable and courageous. This book is for leaders who know that living in a multicultural democracy in times of increasing volatility, uncertainty, chaos, and ambiguity (a VUCA world) requires a different approach to leadership.

This book is for *you* if you know that business as usual is broken and are ready to acknowledge that you have a bigger role to play in the world. If you know that our cascading crises demand something entirely new be born both inside of you and outside in the world, then you're in the right place.

As such, this book attempts to bridge two worlds: our current world that is oppressive, exploitative, and violent, where wealth and power are increasingly concentrated in the hands of a few—and a world that is purposeful, connected, just, creative, equitable, and prosperous. It attempts to bridge humanism and capitalism, empathy and achievement, by leveraging new mechanisms to heal, empower, and unify us. This book is for leaders who want to sleep well at night, proud of how they are newly showing up each day: on purpose, intent on remaking our troubled world. This book is a resource for leaders who want to do just that: fulfill their legacy, activate the higher purpose of their organization, and play a critical role in tending the powerful purpose of these United States.

Luckily, as fate has it, the private sector has many powerful tools to do all of this and more. Yes, there are many things our governments, religions, and schools have done, are doing, and can do. This book is not for people working in those fields, but rather about what each of us working in the private sector can do to fulfill our nation's powerful purpose. It's a guidebook for leaders who want to harvest rich meaning from their careers, activate their purpose, and enjoy soulful connection, kinship, and belonging at work.

Conversely, if you're looking for a book that will help you get ahead or gain an advantage, this ain't it. In general, I hate business books. I find them largely to be a collection of capitalist fan fiction written by folks who don't really understand the central narratives of human history, our nation, and capitalism. Thus, a basic business book cannot remedy the deep flaws embedded within our current arrangements, nor see the power and possibility of capitalism done right. If you'd prefer to avoid or deny our troubled past and present, then this book will upset you.

This book is also a tactical guide for leaders who were intrigued by the possibilities for personal and societal renewal outlined in my previous book, *Planet on Purpose* (2018). This book weaves together four threads: 1. the dream of our nation, 2. stories of reckoning with our nation's past and present on the job, 3. an exploration of what is emerging in the hearts of leaders, employees, customers, and investors, and 4. best practices for leadership and people development in these uncertain times.

This book is for leaders who love our nation. However, we can't fully love something if we don't understand it. Specifically, we often overlook the gap between our ideals and practices, feel the pain in the gap, and see the possibility of closing it. Loving something is not just about celebrating what is great, but critically examining what is unhealed, hurting, and standing in the way of its destiny. It's adopting the posture of Aretha Franklin, U2, or Johnny Cash when they celebrate our nation's richness, glory, and freedom while remaining critical of her failures and advocating for healing, justice, and restitution.

Although this book was written primarily for leaders within the United States, it is also for leaders and people everywhere. What ails us, ails the world. We're all drunk on the same flawed history and the exploitative and unimaginative future it keeps creating. Fascism and authoritarianism are not just on the rise in our nation, they are activated globally[14]. As of 2020, 68% of the world's population now lives under autocratic rule, up from 48% in 2010[15]. While democracy is not a new idea, it's never been tested at the scale of the United States. And it is currently failing, both at home and abroad. Because climate change, nuclear arsenals, extremism, and pandemics threaten our ability to live together on this great Earth–and autocrats pursue self interest above the interest of the collective we will all lose if we let autocracy win.

We must not. All of human life depends on constitutional democracy winning.

Constitutional democracy is not an idea that came from our founders, but from the world's soul, from the deepest part of our psyche: our moral imagination. It's ideals and practices are sourced in a global dialogue extending at least as far back as the Greeks, Tlaxcalans, and Algonquins. Accordingly, we are playing this game not just for the millions living in the United States, but on behalf of all people, past, present, and future. While our influence is not what it was after WWII, the ideas of freedom, equality, and prosperity that we aspire to continue to capture the world's moral imagination.

There is a reason Bruce Springsteen sold twice as many albums internationally as he did in the States. It's the same reason that President Obama was awarded the Nobel Peace Prize in the first year of his presidency despite not being a notable humanitarian or accomplished legislator.

President Obama won the presidency and Nobel Peace Prize and *The Boss* became popular around the globe because deep down, the world needs the United States to fulfill its purpose.

Although President Obama is by no means perfect, he embodies the American Promise. He is living proof that a nation of settler colonialists, descendants of the formerly enslaved, survivors of native genocide, and people from all corners of the globe, can constitute themselves according to sacred ideas—that we can become a place where anyone–no matter their skin color, who they love, how they worship, or who their daddy is–can fulfill their destiny and belong. *Truly belong.*

President Obama gave voice to this deep desire. He performed the sacred task of voicing the deep call for freedom and transmuting *pluribus* into *unum,* 4 years before his presidency began, in his famous 2004 DNC Convention speech:

"...there is not a liberal America and a conservative America—there is the United States of America. There is not a Black America and a white America and Latino America and Asian America—there's the United States of America. The pundits like to slice-and-dice our country into Red States and Blue States; Red States for Republicans, Blue States for Democrats. But I've got news for them, too: We worship an awesome God in the Blue States, and we don't like federal agents poking around in our libraries in the Red States. We coach Little League in the Blue States, and, yes, we've got some gay friends in the Red States. There are patriots who opposed the war in Iraq and there are patriots who supported the war in Iraq...

It's the hope of slaves sitting around a fire singing freedom songs. The hope of immigrants setting out for distant shores. The hope of a young naval lieutenant bravely patrolling the Mekong Delta. The hope of a mill worker's son who dares to defy the odds. The hope of a skinny kid with a funny name who believes that America has a place for him, too. Hope! Hope in

17

the face of difficulty! Hope in the face of uncertainty! The audacity of hope! In the end, that is God's greatest gift to us, the bedrock of this nation. A belief in things not seen. A belief that there are better days ahead."

He continued this provocation in his 2008 victory speech:

"And to all those watching tonight from beyond our shores, from parliaments and palaces to those who are huddled around radios... our stories are singular, but our destiny is shared... Tonight, we proved once more that the true strength of our nation comes not from the might of our arms or the scale of our wealth, but from the enduring power of our ideals: democracy, liberty, opportunity, and unyielding hope.

For that is the true genius of America—that America can change. Our union can be perfected. And what we have already achieved gives us hope for what we can and must achieve tomorrow...

...that fundamental truth that out of many, we are one; that while we breathe, we hope, and where we are met with cynicism, and doubt, and those who tell us that we can't, we will respond with that timeless creed that sums up the spirit of a people: Yes, we can."

Yes we can. This nation's ideals are captured in our defiant "No!" to oppression of any kind and an embodied "Yes!" to freedom, equality, and prosperity. *For all.*

Unfortunately, the lion's share of humanity's potential is being suppressed by oppressive political and economic regimes. Shockingly, 80% of the world's workforce is disengaged[16]. Consider all the amazing things that the 20% of us who are engaged at work have created. Now multiply that by 5. That's what's possible when we ignite purpose, belonging, and flourishing worldwide for all.

Imagine 8,000,000,000 fully-activated souls making their highest contributions, exploring the unknown, celebrating the wonders of nature and community, mining the depths of our collective wisdom, and unleashing our unlimited fount of creativity. *It begins with us.* All people are created equal. *E Pluribus Unum.* Life, liberty, and the pursuit of happiness.

Let's fight like hell to protect and expand this promise for ourselves and for the world!

Author's Note #4: How to Read this Book

Of course you know how to read a book. However, this book does require a bit more emotional effort than most, as we will move through some very charged subjects that will call into question issues concerning identity, capitalism, power, violence, and injustice. So please be kind to yourself, take breaks, and talk to trusted friends and mentors about what you're experiencing. If you feel your wellbeing is declining, please stop reading the book and reach out to a mental health practitioner. To that end, I recommend you read this book with a group of 3-6 people and share your experiences with each other. At the end of each chapter I've included a summary and discussion questions to guide your conversation.

Additionally, there is a group of leaders engaging with this work and bringing it into their organizations. The *Purpose Work Nation* community where you can engage to tap group wisdom, ask questions, share ideas and resources, and receive support for creating cultural and organizational change. You can learn more here: http://purposework.us.

As you move into the latter half of the book, you'll see opportunities to start taking new actions in your organization. This can be scary for the aforementioned reasons, but also because there are often many factors to consider—such as risks to your livelihood, housing, and healthcare, and difficult personalities to navigate—that require a considered approach. To that end, if you want to be in the inquiry of how to take wizened action, please reach out to my team at Unity Lab, as this is familiar territory for us. Please email us at support@unitylab.co.

Author's Note #5: Statement of Privilege

As I am a white man, I speak from my experience and, therefore, cannot possibly hope to offer words that will speak to, inspire, and unify everybody. There's no way I can fully understand the experience of anyone else but myself. While I read and listen to diverse voices and try to understand and embrace alternative perspectives, I'm never going to really "get" the experience of 400 years of racial oppression or millenia of sexist oppression. Although I've received incredible feedback and help on this book from many generous souls who aren't heterosexual white men, there is no escaping my white male perspective and privilege. At the end of the day, I own that. I also recognize that my privilege comes with responsibilities—to use my privilege for the greatest benefit of others.

Additionally, as a white man, I am a member of a group of people who are over-indexed in leadership positions. As such, I often speak directly to the implicit whiteness and maleness inside our economic arrangements and leadership ethos–the internalized, white male perspective embedded, to varying degrees, in all leaders, as well as in capitalism, culture, and our nation as a whole. This is to say that I hope that leaders who identify as women, or who are from the BIPOC or LGBTQIA+ communities, will also find value here. My goal is not to exclude anyone, but rather to speak directly to those who currently hold the power, wealth, and networks that must be leveraged to create a flourishing nation.

Author's Note #6: Privacy Statement

Many names referenced in the stories I tell have been changed to protect the privacy of my friends and colleagues.

Opening Quotes

"...one day this nation will rise up and live out the true meaning of its creed."

–Dr. Martin Luther King, Jr.

"Somehow we've weathered and witnessed
a nation that isn't broken
but simply unfinished...
To compose a country committed to all cultures, colors, characters, and
conditions of man
And so we lift our gazes not to what stands between us
but what stands before us.
We close the divide because we know, to put our future first,
we must first put our differences aside...
But while democracy can be periodically delayed
it can never be permanently defeated..."

–Amanda Gorman

Introduction

"Hey, Mike. Good to see you."

"So, what's up with Black people?!"

(Pause. Shock. Squirm.)

I was speaking with a CEO after his organization had just completed a multi-session anti-racism program. We had developed a connection during the training, and I offered to meet with him about my own journey towards allyship. To hear these words from him after the powerful program we had all experienced together made me wonder what feelings he had about Black people before the training.

It was the summer of 2020. Black Lives Matter (#BLM) protests were sweeping the globe, and companies were scrambling to both demonstrate support for #BLM, and give serious attention to diversity, equity, and inclusion (DEI). DEI budgets ballooned, and by September 2020, there were over 100,000 open DEI positions on LinkedIn. In part, our engagement at Mike's organization was a result of George Floyd's tragic murder and the moral awakening that men like us had after witnessing it.

I would discover, over the course of our conversations, that he wanted to make sense of the racial unrest and the impoverished state of many BIPOC communities, and find a way to express his commitment to inclusion without abandoning his conservative identity. Mike was looking for coherence and a path forward. He valued individualism and personal responsibility, and was having trouble squaring it with his new knowledge of the role that systemic racism plays in tilting the tables against Black folks.

Mike was also a consumer of media that had been painting #BLM as a violent, lesbian, socialist, domestic terror organization, and suggesting that Anti-fa supporters were both fragile snowflakes, and also, magically, a dangerous domestic terror organization. Both assertions have been proven false. Further, 93% of 2020 protests were not violent[1]. To activate one's allyship in the face of the disinformation coming out of traditional and social media organizations in 2020 was a difficult task. It would be far easier to look the other way.

More importantly, he was beginning to see how a lack of inclusion was morally abhorrent to him as an American and a man of faith. Nowhere is it written in the Bible, Torah, Quran, Tao Te Ching, Bhagavad Gita, or Upanishads, that a human life is unworthy of dignity, acceptance, and equal opportunity. Indeed these sacred texts say some version of the opposite.

I could feel the tension in his heart. On one hand, he wanted all the #BLM stuff, the protests, the riots, the lawsuits, etc. to just go away; and on the other hand, he knew it couldn't until justice was served and equity was achieved. I learned that deep down, Mike felt leading inclusively was a personal expression of his Christian faith, his values, and his citizenship. He was called into service on this front, but unsure how to square it with his conservative beliefs, the expectations of his board, and pressure from investors.

We know he's not alone. 90% of white men place some value on DEI, with 42% believing it is very or extremely important to them[2]. Many of these 42% who deeply believe DEI is important, simply do not know how to support it. Less than half of these true believers have ever confronted anyone about an exclusionary comment or behavior, and most have not voluntarily joined an employee resource group (ERG).

Many of us want to see the world improve, but are unsure how or where to begin. In light of the prevailing over-work / always on / rat race ethos of America's work culture, plus the endless pressure from board members and investors to beat earnings estimates, along with organizational inertia, ignoring the call is understandable. It's understandable to want to look away from this fact: if success was only about hard work, then the executive suite would look like a Benetton ad and first generation immigrants would rule the world. How much longer can we look away?

Historically, the few leaders who courageously answered a call to create inclusive cultures and activate the purpose of the United States, frequently failed. Consider that the last two decades of DEI (hiring quotas, mentoring programs, ERG's, mandatory bias training, anonymous reporting systems, etc.) have failed to produce results for our BIPOC, female, and LGBTQIA+ team members. A 2016 Harvard Business Review study of the DEI efforts of 800 organizations revealed that, on the whole, the field delivered neutral to negative outcomes[3]. And, this is after sinking $8 billion a year into DEI[4].

In part, this failure was due to the moralizing and compliance-driven nature of traditional DEI, which made people in power (mostly straight white men) feel attacked. This phenomenon triggers the "complainer effect" where people who are called out get defensive[5].

So, leaders are right to be careful as they inclusively develop their cultures. And yet, this is the tension. Leaders know that culture matters and they can no longer stay silent on social issues. Sixty-two% of adults now demand that companies take a stand on social, economic, and environmental issues[6], and 87% of consumers believe business should put just as much attention on social issues as economic results[7].

They've also seen culture issues torpedo mergers and acquisitions (M+A) and other critical strategies, and be the source of scandal and corruption. They've seen the results of missed hiring, retention, and performance goals. They've seen top talent flee for startups and organizations with inclusive cultures, great Glassdoor ratings, and B Corp designations.

Leaders are stuck between taking the traditional laissez faire approach to culture—ensuring the same white guys get hired and promoted, resulting in lawsuits, missed targets, and customer and employee churn—and actively crafting culture, which will take a bunch of time and money, and is unlikely to succeed under the current DEI paradigm. Until very recently, this was an unsolvable tension.

In 2020, my colleague, Christina Asbaty, and I co-authored a research study[8] in partnership with Golden Gate University, to measure and assess a unique culture change method with a global biotechnology company with 50k+ employees. This method involved forming small, diverse, peer-learning groups who committed to learning something together over time. We saw outstanding results: 95% course completion (versus 5% industry completion rate[9]), 85% behavior change and 76% new daily habit formation rates. Further, 98% of participants experienced respect from their diverse peers, 96% experienced empathy from their diverse peers, and women and BIPOC employees reported increases in organizational commitment of 11.3% and 13.6%, respectively.

When this method is used to activate employees' purpose (As a reminder I define purpose as a transcendent identity beyond the concerns of self and family that includes many aspects such as: one's vision for the world, mission, craft, greatest gifts, and most cherished values; for a deeper dive into the 10 aspects of purpose, the purpose activation process, and purposeful leadership, see my previous book, *Planet on Purpose*) at work, both people and organizations thrive, as purpose is correlated with:

- 175% increase in productivity[10]
- 63% increase in leadership effectiveness[11]
- 30% increase in innovation[12]
- 4x reduction in anxiety in diverse environments[13]
- 7.4 months in additional tenure[14]

New tools and approaches are now available for leaders to achieve their performance goals and reduce risk and employee turnover by activating purpose and belonging in small, diverse peer-learning groups. In doing so, they also activate our nation's purpose by nurturing relationships across gender, political, and racial differences.

Before we explore this proven pathway, we'll need to lay down the foundation. Broadly, this book is divided into two parts. Chapters 1-3 are more historical and philosophical, examining the purpose, history, challenges, and opportunities facing our nation and organizations. Chapters 4-6 are more tactical, looking at how you can lead your organization into a flourishing future and steward the nation's purpose.

We'll begin by looking at why organizations are the front line in the fight for our nation's purpose (Chapter 1). In short, America is deeply segregated racially, economically, geographically, generationally, and politically, and the workplace is where we have the best opportunity to connect across boundaries and share a commitment to learn and grow together. We'll also look at a unifying mythology to guide our leadership and nation and the return on investment (ROI) of activating purpose and belonging (Chapter 2). Next, we'll look at the urgent need to shift our culture (Chapter 3).

We'll then explore how the old way of doing Learning and Development (L+D), DEI, Wellness and Culture is a huge waste of time and money, and actually creates greater inequity, division, and disengagement, and how the new way—building authentic, high-trust, and diverse relationships across an organization—delivers better results and enables unprecedented productivity, innovation, well-being, information transfer, and organizational commitment (Chapter 4). We'll then dive deeper into the two most powerful drivers of organizational flourishing: purpose and belonging (Chapter 5). We'll conclude with an approach (Chapter 6) for activating a culture of purpose and belonging in your organization.

Let's now begin with an exploration into the past, present, and future possibilities of business in this nation.

Chapter 1

Business as Religion, Villain, and Savior

"It's the only way to treat a white man."

(laughter)

I was 16 when I heard these words. I'm ashamed to admit it now, but I joined in the laughter and nodded in agreement. We had just finished a round of golf at my all-male and almost all-white country club (except for a few Japanese businessmen with whom we never interacted). We were sitting around a card table, smoking cigars, and watching sports. Tony, the Cuban bartender, had just brought us our drinks. A friend of my father then said those lamentable words and we all laughed. I didn't think anything of it and we continued our conversation.

In the 20th century, clubs like this one were where business got done. The relationships that form in these aristocratic enclaves–from the yacht and golf clubs around our cities, to the town clubs such as the Harvard Club in New York, the University Club in Chicago, and the Olympic Club in San Francisco–have been the engine oil of business. This is not to say you couldn't do business without belonging to such a club; it was just a lot easier as a member, as trust was assumed among members within each club, and between the members of these clubs via reciprocal guest agreements. My dad made his living managing the wealth of many of our club's members. I was counseled to do the same: hang out with rich, white people, ingratiate yourself, and do business with them.

Business as Religion

There was no sense of anything lost or wrong in joining or wanting to join these exclusive and primarily white male communities. As the thinking went, what was good for business was good for the nation. And, business just happened to be done by white men, so successful white businessmen became our revered clergy. Men like Michael Milken, Jack Welch, Warren Buffett, and Ted Turner adorned magazine covers, bought jets and estates, and offered us a gospel of prosperity.

During my childhood, our economy was credited with defeating the Third Reich and the U.S.S.R. and putting a washing machine in every home and a car in every driveway. There was an implied nobility in it, and it never bothered us that women or BIPOC folks weren't among our revered clergy or benefited from it. Our post-WWII prosperity and Milton Friedman's "the business of business is business" battle cry empowered us to pursue profit as a moral good. It meant we had a moral license to do whatever was necessary to expand profits, thus sanctioning our discriminatory, anti-labor, and environmentally disastrous business practices. As far as I knew, capitalism was the best of all possible worlds.

Of course, I wanted to fit in, did not know any better, and so I followed the path laid out before me. I picked one of the whitest majors (finance), joined a white fraternity, poured drinks at a white bar, dated white sorority women, played sports, made the Dean's List, and held leadership positions. Like most of my fraternity brothers, I wanted to be successful, and used college as a resume polisher for my default white male destiny: a career in white professional services, a house in the white suburbs, complete with a white housewife, 2.3 white kids, membership at a white country club and a white church.

> **WARNING:** The following section contains some hard truths. It's bitter, but vital medicine. Every leader must understand the broad strokes of how we got here in order to effectively lead in an increasingly diverse and volatile economy. The last 40 years of historical research has revealed a vastly different story of the nation and capitalism than the version we were likely taught. We're going to cover a portion of it here to prepare a solid foundation of our nation's history and economy. So, if you discover facts new to you, please explore the source material in the endnotes, as well as consider reading David Graeber and David Wengrow's *The Dawn of Everything*, Howard Zinn's *The People's History of the United States*, Nikole Hannah Jones' *The 1619 Project: A New Origin Story*, and Roxanne Dunbar-Ortiz's *An Indigenous People's History of the United States*. As mentioned in the Author's Notes, please be kind to yourself, take breaks and seek support if necessary.

Business as Villain

Success in business in the 1980s meant wealth, luxury, and subsistence-wage servants. To bring us drinks. Mow our lawns. Clean our houses. Wash and valet our cars. Carry our bags. Raise our kids. Make our food. The weird thing was that no one talked about it. No one seemed to notice that, if you squinted your eyes, the Chicago suburbs looked a lot like southern plantations with mostly white homeowners and mostly BIPOC service providers. Not that I was privy to overt malice or secret meetings, but the centuries' old relationship between white folks and the BIPOC "help" continued.

While it was working out pretty well for us, it obviously wasn't working out for Black folks. Black men earn $.56[1] and Black women earn $.63 for every $1 a white man earns[2], and Black families have $.01 wealth for every dollar a white family has[3]. Although I was not aware that anyone actively sought to oppress and exploit people of color or women, the net effect of our jobs, biases, marriages, and our suburban lifestyles did exactly that.

"I'm not saying that white people are better. I'm saying that being white is clearly better, who could even argue? If it was an option, I would re-up every year. 'Oh yeah I'll take white again absolutely, I've been enjoying that, I'll stick with white, thank you.'"

— Louis CK, 2008

Our collective actions (giving contracts and jobs to mostly other white guys, NIMBY-ism, and cutting taxes, education, and social services that disproportionately benefit women, children, the elderly, and BIPOC folks) ensured that we kept the power and wealth for ourselves, while women and people of color made a lot less money serving us. Younger folks are now making us feel more uncomfortable about it, but nothing has really changed.

Granted, we do have increasing diversity in boardrooms, media, and political leadership, and overtly racist attitudes have declined substantially[4]. Unfortunately, our country remains structurally segregated: geographically, politically, racially, and generationally. How did it become this way?

Divide, dehumanize, dominate, and dispossess has been our way since "go"[5,6,7]. Since the first ships of settler colonialists arrived on Turtle Island, our legacy has been one of exploitation for profit. This is not to diminish what is good, true, and beautiful about our religions, culture, technologies, and art, but rather to shed light upon our nation's shadow, and incorporate a central theme of our legacy and political economy that is frequently ignored or resisted. We need to see the whole map if we are to understand who we are, how we got here, and in what manner we should proceed. This is also not to romanticize African or First Nations people who also had political maneuvering, fierce warriors, injustices, slavery, and torture.

However, what the First Nations had, but our settler, colonialist ancestors did not—besides a rightful claim to Turtle Island—were intact cultures, in which war, peace, spirituality, politics, economics, culture, love, and friendship existed in relative harmony both within each nation and between them, and with the earth and the Great Spirit. What they had was a general regard for personal sovereignty, especially that of women and children, and the prolific ability to invent dozens of social, political, and economic arrangements to maximize freedom, sovereignty, and flourishing.

What First Nations had was an understanding of property that included the responsibility to care for it, versus the European notion of property rights, whose origins are rooted in the laws of the Roman Empire, granting the right to use, enjoy, abuse, and destroy one's land, animals and people at will, and use violence towards any threat to one's property. This master-slave ethos is still guiding our language, culture, organizations, legal system, employee contracts, and moral reasoning. For example, consider these Latin words: *familus* referring to the slaves and servants of a household, from where get family and familiar; *dominus*, from which we get domicile and dominate; *capitalis*, meaning head, chief or first; and *labor*, meaning hardship, pain, toil, and fatigue. All refer to our need to distinguish the dominator from the dominated (land, people, animals, and property).

Conversely, First Nations people enjoy a more mutualistic coherence between their people, cosmologies, politics, cultures, economies, and Mother Earth. This symbiosis results in an enormous sense of belonging, meaning, security, and ease. In an only recently unearthed 1942 paper from Abraham Maslow, we now have a view rooted in Western psychology for understanding what the cultures and personalities of the original caretakers of this land might have been like.

Maslow spent the summer of 1938 with the Blackfoot people in Alberta, Canada, one of the few relatively intact native communities at the time. These people had yet to be decimated by poverty, alcohol, and the assimilation policies of the Canadian government and Christianity. Maslow found a society marked by remarkable freedom, self-esteem, and security; he surmised that 70-80% of the Blackfoot people were more secure than the top 5% most secure Westerners. He discovered that they had:

"...feelings of being liked and loved; the perception of the world as a warm and friendly place; a tendency to expect good to happen; feelings of calm, ease, and relaxation; self-acceptance; a desire for adequacy with respect to problems rather than for power over people; 'social interest' (in the Adlerian sense); cooperativeness; kindliness; interest in others; and sympathy... Children are not humiliated by their parents as they are in our society... Inferior men are not humiliated by superior men, nor are the poor humiliated by the rich... The typical personality of the Northern Blackfoot Indian is one characterized by dignity and friendliness and containing little insecurity, suspicion, envy, jealousy, antagonism and hostility or anxiety..."[8]

It is, perhaps, not surprising that, when invading settler colonialists were captured by natives and given the opportunity to leave, they chose to stay among the natives. Even captured children, when confronted by their biological parents, chose to stay with their indigenous captors[9]. As Benjamin Franklin observed,

"...when white persons of either sex have been taken prisoner young by the Indians, and lived awhile among them, tho' ransomed by their Friends, and treated with all imaginable tenderness to prevail with them to stay among the English, yet in a short time they become disgusted with our manner of life, and the care and pains that are necessary to support it, and take the first opportunity of escaping again into the Woods, from whence there is no reclaiming them."[10]

Further, many of the 18th century ideas and practices we attribute to European intellectuals and upon which our nation's founding documents rest—such as liberty, equality, deliberative democracy, and societal critique—were observed by Europeans in their 16th century discussions with Indigenous leaders[11]. Additionally, we owe to First Nations people many fields of inquiry and practices that we've only recently begun to explore, such as depth psychology, restorative justice, regenerative land management, public housing, and the sovereignty of women and children[12]. Of course, we did not deliver upon these ideas as the First Nations did. In practice, we took what we could comprehend through our master-slave / "power over others" worldview, and left the rest.

This ethos continued as we set upon the continent of Africa to steal, traffic, enslave, murder, rape, and torture their people, resulting in a total of 4,000,000 enslaved people by 1860[13]. Given that the average lifespan of an enslaved person at the time was 10-36 years[14], depending on their conditions and the duration of the practice, it is likely that the number of people we dehumanized, dominated, and dispossessed is many times that number.

To prevent worker and enslaved uprisings, we needed to prevent solidarity between poor Europeans, First Nations people and those we enslaved. And so we invented the concept of "whiteness" to give poor Europeans a class distinction, moral license, and economic roles, such as strike breakers, slave patrols, and forward rangers, to keep the native "frontier" moving west, ensure relative "peace" in the east, and keep our forced labor camps running smoothly[15]. These forces, composed largely of Scots-Irish, eventually morphed into the police and military forces we know today. The impact, while different in tactics, is eerily familiar: dehumanize, divide, dominate, and dispossess those who have something we want.

We also gave incentives to wealthier white men to enslave Africans by awarding an extra 75 acres of land for every person they enslaved, which resulted in a hugely profitable influx of the enslaved who both worked the land and built our nation's public infrastructure. Broadway was cleared by those we enslaved. Canals were dredged and roads, sewers, and bridges were built by the enslaved. The wall from which Wall St. was named, the White House, and the Capitol were all built by those we enslaved. Citi and J.P. Morgan financed the trade of the enslaved, and accepted enslaved humans as collateral. Aetna and New York Life insured the trade[16].

With our domestic exploitation project nearing completion in the 19th century, we turned our gaze towards Latin America and the South Pacific, and then in the 20th, to the rest of the world. A reading of the last 100 years of U.S. foreign policy reveals that we have done little but preach about democracy and human rights, while undermining and impoverishing other countries with expensive debt, overthrowing their legitimate governments, assassinating their leaders, drone-striking insurgents and innocent bystanders, installing corrupt puppets friendly to U.S. business interests, and then bullying them to sell us their labor and natural resources for pennies on the dollar. As of 2022, U.S. foreign policy has interfered in the elections and power structures in 80 countries[17].

It is, of course, a great shame that we ginned up countless narratives that First Nations and foreign people were backwards, in order to justify war, theft, genocide, slavery, oppression, and interventionism. And, like the Roman Empire, we did not save our worst behavior for foreign people; we also maintained our ethos of "divide and conquer" at home.

We use our sharp elbows to pay subsistence wages, beat the competition, find the angle, maximize return, plunder nature, "get the girl," lock up the "bad guys", "make it rain", and isolate children, the elderly, and the infirm. As anyone who has ever been to high school knows, it's not just white people oppressing non-white people, it's everyone oppressing everyone else.

It is our history, identity, and practice. Whether we look at ourselves as a country of:

- 1 master race,
- 2 genders,
- 3 lifestyles: urban, suburban, rural,
- 4 distinct political attitudes: Real America (e.g., Sarah Palin), Free America (e.g., Milton Friedman), Smart America (e.g., Sheryl Sandberg), and Just America (e.g., Angela Davis)[18],
- 5 distinct generations: Zenials, Millennials, Gen X, Baby Boomers, Silent Generation[19],
- 12 distinct socioeconomic communities, as Dante Chinni and James Gimpel offer in *Our Patchwork Nation* (2012), or
- Our 100's of ethnicities...

We are a divided nation.

The result is that 74% of us don't have any friends from different ethnicities, 69% of us don't have any friends from different generations, 63% of us don't have any friends with different levels of education, 62% of us don't have any friends who vote differently, and 56% don't have any friends from different income brackets[20]. It appears that white folks are the most segregated group, as 92% of people in the networks of white people are white[21]. And, it is getting worse, as our education system is increasingly segregated along the lines of race, class, and politics[22]. Over half of our children now attend deeply segregated schools[23].

Unfortunately, when we divide and blame each other, we miss the deeper dehumanizing narrative of our story, not to mention the shared shame, suffering, and hopelessness we all feel because of it. We also miss the power of owning our history and the solidarity we could harness to live our nation's purpose and dream a better future together. Of course, there is good reason to keep dividing and blaming each other. The implications of this history are unpleasant, to say the least.

So that we can own our history and create a new future, let us now turn to the phrase that describes our past and present: "white supremacy." Many of our divides overlap and enforce a dynamic of "Christian, white male, ableist, heteronormative supremacy," or for short, "white supremacy." Today, being part of a white supremacist system doesn't just mean lynching and burning crosses, although there are 10 million citizens with white nationalist / insurrectionist sympathies[24], and a few thousand white nationalists still actively perpetuating domestic terrorism upon our fellow citizens of Jewish, African, Hispanic, Indigenous, Muslim, and Asian descent. It means that we all participate—regardless of how we vote, work, worship, or love—in an interlocking system that keeps wealthy white families on top, and deprives others of their rights, dignity, and the fruits of their labor.

As Robin DiAngelo offers, white supremacy is comprised of dozens, if not hundreds, of explicit and implicit beliefs about whiteness and non-whiteness that have been codified into institutional laws and norms that govern every sector of our society, including and especially our economy:

"White supremacy captures the all-encompassing centrality and assumed superiority of people defined and perceived as white, and the practices based upon that assumption. White supremacy is not simply the idea that whites are superior to people of color (although it certainly is that), but a deeper premise that supports this idea—the definition of whites as the norm or standard for *human*, and people of color as an inherent deviation from that norm…

"We use the term to refer to a socio-political economic system of domination based on racial categories that benefit those defined and perceived as white. This system rests on the historical and current accumulation of structural power that privileges, centralizes, and elevates white people as a group."[25]

While it is no longer a conspiracy by Romans, monarchs, barons, or slavers, it continues because of our fear, ignorance, and lack of moral imagination. It is the water we swim in. It's why luxury cars and strip clubs exist. It's why Jack Welch boasted about culling the bottom 10% of GE, and why women live in constant fear of sexual assault. It's why the hidden becomes visible when enough angry white folks get together (e.g., when students at a Connecticut prep school wrote "Kill All N@#$%&s" in their yearbook in 1995[26], why Yalies marched on campus in 2010 chanting, "No means 'yes', 'yes' means anal"[27], and why the Unite the Right rally in Charleston in 2017 chanted "Jews will not replace us!"[28]).

Its form and expression keep changing, but its impact remains. It has evolved from war against women, children, the elderly, First Nations, and African peoples, and into laws and practices such as the ⅗ compromise, broken treaties, Black Codes, deporting over 1,000,000 U.S. citizens of Mexican descent in the 1920s and 1930s, contract lending, Chinese and Japanese internment camps, Jim Crow laws, Sundown towns, payday loans, redlining, police brutality, and the preschool to prison pipeline[29].

"Racism is like a Cadillac, they bring out a new model every year."

- Malcolm X

What else can explain why Black families only have $.01 of wealth for every dollar a white family has? We'd have to say that there is something deficient in Black people or their culture, which is both explicitly racist, and factually incorrect-in fact, it can be argued that much of our nation's finest writing, music, legislation, science, technology, athletics, art, spirituality, and cuisine came from the minds, bodies, and souls of Black folks-or we'd have to admit that our system creates better outcomes for white people as a function of the system, not as a bug in the system. If we admit the former, at least we would be factually correct.

Now comes the hard part. We must acknowledge that, regardless of our racial, ethnic, religious, or class status, we depend on a white supremacist and ecocidal system to survive, and that "staying out of it" or doing nothing to change it is a vote in favor of it. Remaining neutral ensures that no matter how hard our fellow citizens from BIPOC communities try, they will not succeed; eventually they will be forced by the market to serve wealthy whites. Staying neutral is not just a vote for further oppression and biosphere collapse, but is also an assault upon our national purpose and our wild-eyed, rambunctious nature, as anthropologist Margaret Mead observed...

"[We] ...have no tolerance at all of anybody putting up with anything. We believe that whatever is going wrong ought to be fixed."

While it's understandable to not want to face our past and present, it is dishonorable to make the inquiry itself wrong (e.g., ignore it, ban it, deflect, engage in doublespeak, or cancel people). A true leader is willing to have the discussion, accept the facts, admit her wrongs, face his accuser, make satisfactory amends, ensure further harm ceases, and call forth a future of collective flourishing. A true leader is willing to look at the data we've explored (in addition to the data concerning climate change, which is also deeply concerning[30]). Until recently, few leaders have been willing to embrace the data and answer the call.

Answering the call is a hard and long road. Due to the volatility and competition in our economy, little time to observe and reflect, along with the great fear of screwing it up or sounding unhinged, it is tempting to lower our sights on what is possible. It's easy to snack on small, surface-level wins like science fair exhibits about climate change, and diverse TV shows, board members, entertainers, Olympians, politicians, and scholarship winners. It's easy to comfort ourselves by saying "It's not as bad as it used to be" and deflect responsibility. And, it's uncomfortable to face the fact that, while our rhetoric has become more humane and inclusive, the operating system has not been updated. We're still burning our house down. We're still oppressing. Structural racism is alive and well, making life considerably less free or equitable for BIPOC folks today than it was 50 years ago[31].

If we continue to ignore, and thus damage, our powerful purpose, we do so not just at the expense of the flourishing of our BIPOC sisters and brothers and our biosphere, but also at the expense of white flourishing as well. White people are also hustling for subsistence wages and struggling with obesity, addiction, and lack of affordable education and healthcare. White families also don't have clean air, water, and food. White children are also struggling with fear, anxiety, depression, and suicide. White people also have trouble sleeping. White parents are also burnt out and stretched thin. White people are also being raped.

Had we been guided by our shared purpose to face and heal our history, and expanded the social and economic policies of the 1940s, 50s, and 60s, and followed the climate science of the last 40 years, then we all would be better off. For example, by addressing racism head on, we would have generated an additional $16T in our economy over the last 2 decades[32].

In 2022, living our nation's purpose means making a living wage, which is $25-50/hour[33] with less than a 30-minute commute. It means affordable healthcare (<5% of income). It means being part of a safe, loving, stable, and inclusive community. It means access to clean water, air, and soil. It means healthy and affordable food. It means small class sizes. It means sustainable and affordable public transit and housing (<25% of income). It means being free from oppression and having the right to vote. It means we do not get roofied and raped, nor murdered by police during a routine traffic stop. As we've explored, this is not our lived experience.

Well, at least we have each other to lean on in our despair. Nope.

Even more than being divided into groups, within these groups, we frequently suffer alone. Only 47% of us belong to a spiritual community, down from 70% in 1999[34]; 61% of us are lonely, up from 46% just a few years ago[35]; 33% of us have only 1-3 close friends and 17% of us have no close friends at all—double the number from 2013[36]. 41% of us don't have a best friend, up from 23% in 1995[37]; and trust in our fellow citizens has fallen to 32% from 57% in 1968[38]. Further, this dynamic seems to be impacting men disproportionately, in what has been called a "male friendship recession," the number of men reporting zero friends has increased 5 times since 1995[39].

Given that we laugh 5 times less when we're alone versus with others[40], the more alone we are, the more our "pursuit of happiness" is unrealized. As you might imagine, this dynamic creates all sorts of mental health issues. 8.5% of us are depressed, with 32.8% of us reporting an increase of depressive symptoms in 2021[41]. In 2013, 1 in 6 of us took an antidepressant—3 times as many who did in 1996[42].

This dynamic is especially crushing for our youth who have come of age in this era. Although they have an abundance of consumer choices, they grew up watching their parents check out and their leaders sell them out. They watched helplessly as leaders burned their planet, raised their tuitions, killed unions, offshored jobs, decimated our Main Street downtowns, and flattened wages. With little hope that anyone is looking out for them, they freaked out. In the 1990s, the average college student was 85% more anxious than those in the 1950s and normal school children in the 1980s had higher levels of anxiety than psychiatric patients in the 1950s[43]. This generalized fear also bleeds into how young people feel about each other. For example, in 1976, 46% of high school students believed "most people can be trusted," which fell to 16% in 2014[44]. Who can blame them?

By 2018, suicide had become the leading cause of death for people 10-24 years of age, and it's getting worse. For example, between 2019 and 2021, suicide attempts among girls aged 12-17 increased 51%. These epidemics have led the American Academy of Pediatrics, American Academy of Child and Adolescent Psychiatry, and the Children's Hospital Association to declare a national emergency in children's mental health[45].

Initially, this meaninglessness, disconnection, fear, and isolation was "good" for business—as the core human needs for purpose and belonging that were traditionally met by family, friends, community service, religion, and relationships formed over years of steady work, could now be readily (although not substantially nor sustainably) sold back to us via an ever-increasing menu of goods and services. Businesses could now make a healthy profit selling us new goods and services to deal with our woes, such as gated communities, social media, streaming services, cheap credit, automatic weapons, security systems, rape kits, air purifiers, private schools, fast fashion, prison contracts, bail bonds, active shooter trainings, payday loans, self-defense classes, pills, and dialysis centers. However, because of the last four decades of flat wages and buying power[46], we are increasingly unable to afford them.

This moment is ripe for populist uprisings. Political entrepreneurs easily exploit our isolation by peeling us off into their ideologies and conspiracy theories that claim to explain and blame away our problems. For many of us, grievance is our common cause; all that binds many of us today is some version of "life sucks and someone is going to pay." As we'll explore in Chapter 3, this has resulted in a "cold civil war" that could turn hot at any minute.

Unfortunately, help isn't coming from D.C. The very people we have hired to enact our purpose and ensure we survive and thrive are on the take. Landmark research at Princeton University on the state of our democracy has revealed that we are a democracy in name only[47]. We are technically an oligarchy, ruled by the wealthy and corporate interests who ensured that their power and wealth expand at the expense of the well-being of our nation's diverse citizenry, democracy, and a liveable world.

Why, in a nation with a purpose as noble as ours, is this happening?

Lots of reasons. 50,000,000,000 to be exact. By cutting taxes for the wealthy and businesses, and decimating unions and programs for everyone else, $50T transferred from the bottom 90% to the top 1% over the last four decades. This means that a college-educated worker earning $72,000 today loses between $48,000 and $63,000 of income per year[48]. In addition to the $16T that racism has cost us, another $50T has been taken from us. Add these two together and we have a $66T loss.

Put another way, we stand to gain what Heather McGhee, author of *The Sum of Us*, might refer to as a $66T "solidarity dividend."[49] If we choose to address and resolve our racial and class divisions, then we will be far better off. Consider that two-thirds of this ($44T) we could be taking home and investing in home down payments, family vacations, preventative healthcare, education, starting a business, or civic organizations. Consider that the other third paid in taxes ($22T) could be invested in a public healthcare option, affordable housing, renewable energy, public transit, small class sizes, and reducing our debt.

However, the oligarchy refuses to rest, and instead, continues to tighten its grip. According to a non-partisan consortium of pro-democracy organizations, 262 restrictive voting bills in 41 states have been introduced since the 2020 election; and as of December 2021, 17 states have enacted 32 new voter suppression laws[50]. As such, it is no wonder that our trust in government has fallen dramatically. Now, only 24% of us trust the government, down from a high of 77% in 1964;[51] and 69% of us believe the government only serves the interests of the wealthy[52].

In other countries, when these dynamics exist, we call it what it is: an apartheid, an oligarchy, or a corporatocracy. We call it anything but an actual democracy. As a result, many of us have lost hope. Although we have spent years and decades trying to achieve some level of security, peace, and ease, our lives are no better for the effort, and in many cases, they are far worse. The "American Dream" no longer fits the data or our lived experience. As such, over half of us now believe it is unattainable[53].

> **SORBET:** With these hard, but necessary truths out of the way, I recommend you cleanse your palette. Do what you need to do to "shake it off." Perhaps take a walk around the block, have a good cry, or seek a hug from a loved one.

Business as Savior

"I think our last best hope is the leadership of the U.S. business community…"

Thomas Friedman, The New York Times, January 4, 2022[54]

There is hope. Although you'd be right to think business would be the last place to turn, it is also in the perfect position to revitalize our purpose, rehumanize our society, save the republic, and regenerate the planet. In fact, organizations are the only place where we have sufficient diversity across race, gender, politics, ethnicity, ability, sexuality, and age, and the substantial and sustained time commitment (2,000 hours per person per year) that is required to build diverse relationships and also transform beliefs and behaviors, as compared to the time we spend in less diverse religious, civic, and neighborhood organizations (10-200 hours per year).

Changing behavior isn't a matter of merely learning new information, but rather a sustained commitment requiring self-inquiry, modeling, practice, support, and the network redundancy[55] that organizations amply provide.

Mechanisms of change must come from multiple people in a network, versus top down, or merely learned in a class, sent out in an email, and painted on a wall. They must be continually modeled, developed, and expanded over time. The good news is that once 25% of a population adopts a belief or behavior, it soon becomes the norm[56].

In a sense, an organization is like a sovereign nation with its origin story, values, mission, and vision; its own economy, media, and culture, with its own education, healthcare, and environmental functions. Further, business knows no borders, has vastly greater resources than any other sector, is unencumbered by term limits or the need to constantly whip up its base with hate and hyperbole.

Additionally, and again paradoxically, business is regarded as the most ethical and competent sector, with 78% of us trusting our employer[57]. There is even greater trust in small businesses (<500 employees), which is where 46.8% of us work[58], and 94% of us trust small businesses to do the right thing[59]. And, what's more, people expect business to lead the way; 68% of us believe business should fill the government's leadership/trust void[60].

Many businesses are starting to understand that future innovation and success don't depend on further extraction and exploitation, but rather on trust, psychological safety, purpose, wellness, sustainability, and collaboration. They know that 89% of people want to live their purpose at work,[61] and that there is only a 1% chance of being fulfilled in life if we're not fulfilled at work[62]. They know how much better they perform when 100% of their employees feel safe, like they belong, can grow, activate their purpose, and do their best work. They all know they cannot operate if the planet can no longer support life.

Especially as artificial intelligence (A.I.) makes the rote and analytical cheap and easy, if there is any hope for our nation, we must remember and reignite what makes us uniquely human: purpose, creativity, and our bonds to each other. To this end, businesses invest heavily in learning and development, spending $367B per year[63], $8B per year in DEI[64], and $57B per year in employee wellness[65]. As we'll explore in Chapter 4, these channels need a drastic revisioning in order to truly serve the needs of employees, organizations, and the nation.

You are likely aware of a few organizations in your industry who are well on their way to rehumanizing their cultures, sustainably reimagining their businesses, and using their brand, voice, and buying power to create a more perfect union. Organizations, such as Ford, Blackrock, LinkedIn, PWC, New Belgium Brewing, Salesforce, Thomson Reuters, AirBNB, and Eileen Fisher Clothing, invest heavily in sustainability, employee purpose, and belonging initiatives. While these companies are by no means perfect, they have chosen to follow the wisdom of Peter Drucker ("Culture eats strategy for breakfast") because they know their cultures cannot serve only one-third of the workforce (white men).

It's needed and it's time. As we'll explore in the next chapter, your employees, customers, and investors now demand it.

Imagine each person you work with being connected to their purpose and to each other, bringing living wages and a sense of belonging and fulfillment back home, impacting the health and resilience of their families, neighborhoods, and ecosystems. Imagine the 20 largest employers in your area doing the same. Imagine the culture and economy of a nation where sustainable and equitable flourishing is the new normal. Imagine 330,000,000 souls activated, curious, creative, caring, and connected. Imagine the sense of fulfillment you will have in helping bring forth this future. These ripple effects are what can make our sacred purpose real.

There is plenty of precedent for business doing the right thing. Business has come to the aid of our democracy many times before. It rose to the challenge in the 1940s to mobilize the economy and defeat Hitler; to defeat anti-LGBTQIA+ legislation in 2015 in Indiana and in 2016 in North Carolina; and to stop selling automatic weapons in 2018 after the Parkland massacre. Because business leaders understand how important a functioning democracy is to the health of their enterprise, following the January 6 attack on the Capitol, hundreds of CEOs called for a second impeachment, paused donations to politicians who supported the attack, and issued a statement denouncing the restrictive voting efforts underway in a majority of our states.

Businesses are being called upon once again. If businesses decide they want to activate *e pluribus unum* and "life, liberty, and the pursuit of happiness" by sustainably reimagining their supply chains, paying living wages, and creating cultures of purpose and belonging, then they can do that. Further, due to their outsized influence in the government, some business leaders have the ear and pocketbook of our public servants. If businesses want to reinstate the FCC Fairness Doctrine to eliminate misleading and partisan news, or amend Section 230 of the Communications Decency Act to make social media companies responsible for the content their algorithms surface, or make sustainable supply chains the law of the land, or provide a public healthcare option, unburdening businesses from the growing hassle and expense of doing it themselves and thereby liberating entrepreneurs and creating greater workforce agility, or ensure teachers are well paid and have small class sizes, or guarantee the right to vote, or see to it that our nation builds a renewable energy infrastructure, then they can do that.

They can do any of it. As the data suggests, it's time to do all of it. Unfortunately, the majority of the business community has been resistant to actively steward the common good.

But, why? In the next chapter, we'll explore the myth that has driven our economy and culture since the beginning, and summon a new myth to guide us into a future of shared and sustainable prosperity.

Chapter 1 Summary:

- In the 20th century, capitalism was regarded as an unqualified moral good.
- The current political economy of the United States fails to fulfill our nation's purpose, and instead creates inequality, division, exploitation, climate change, and human suffering.
- Business is more powerful and trustworthy than the government.
- While this is undoubtedly an "all-hands-on-deck moment" for leaders across sectors, without the leadership of business, at best our nation will remain a languishing, apartheid state, and at worst, the republic will fall and our planet will become unhabitable.

Chapter 1 Reflection Questions:

- What feelings arise as you consider that, despite our powerful purpose, the United States is a white supremacist, ecocidal, apartheid state?
- How have you benefited from white supremacy?
- How have you been constrained or imperiled by white supremacy?
- How would you feel if you shifted your organization to empower everyone to fulfill their potential and flourish?

Chapter 2

The Bison Way

"I have a dream that one day this nation will rise up and live out the true meaning of its creed: 'We hold these truths to be self-evident, that all [people] are created equal.'

I have a dream that one day on the red hills of Georgia, the sons of former slaves and the sons of former slave owners will be able to sit down together at the table of brotherhood.

I have a dream that one day even the state of Mississippi, a state sweltering with the heat of injustice, sweltering with the heat of oppression, will be transformed into an oasis of freedom and justice.

I have a dream that my four little children will one day live in a nation where they will not be judged by the color of their skin but by the content of their character..."

- Martin Luther King, Jr., 1963

While today, we find these words inspiring, at the time of their utterance, they provoked serious resistance and eventually resulted in the murder of Dr. King and many of his contemporaries. In this chapter, we'll look at the deeper theme underlying our resistance to racial and class solidarity, and consider how to actualize our national purpose more broadly.

Every nation has a dream, a code, a unifying myth that evokes its origins, and holds its culture, society, and economy together. The same is true of organizations. As such, if we are to fulfill our purpose as a nation, and understand the role that organizations have in fulfilling it, then we'll have to surface the underlying myth that has driven our nation for centuries and Western civilization since at least the beginning of the Roman Empire (27 BCE). With a sober grasp of this myth, we can evoke a new one. We'll do just that by offering another myth that is older, yet more indigenous, inclusive, inspiring, prosperous, and expressive of our stated purpose and Dr. King's "beloved community."

As we explored in the last chapter, the history and socioeconomics of our nation are markedly different from Dr. King's dream. The myth that guides our nation is that of the rugged individualist (typically, a white man). He overcame the odds through wit, guile, creativity, and determination. He made a name for himself, became wealthy, and fulfilled his destiny. The heroes of our myth are men like Elon Musk, Tom Brady, Thomas Edison, Andrew Carnegie, Warren Buffett, Bill Gates, and John Rockefeller. We praise men like these: the resource extractor, the champion, the inventor, the investor, the technology "disruptor".

I believe this myth is best represented by our national bird, the bald eagle, which was selected after an intense debate by our founders. It makes sense to inquire as to why a solitary bird of prey who sweeps down from on high, who hunts, steals, extracts, and retreats to its perch to savor the feast, was selected to express the spirit of our nation versus a social herd animal.

Perhaps on some unconscious level, it was selected for its colors: a golden beak and white feathers on top and brown feathers on the bottom, much like the distribution of power and wealth at home and what would guide our foreign policy.

> "For my own part I wish the Bald Eagle had not been chosen the Representative of our Country. He is a Bird of bad moral Character. He does not get his Living honestly. You may have seen him perched on some dead Tree near the River, where, too lazy to fish for himself, he watches the Labour of the Fishing Hawk; and when that diligent Bird has at length taken a Fish, and is bearing it to his Nest for the Support of his Mate and young Ones, the Bald Eagle pursues him and takes it from him.
>
> With all this injustice, he is never in good case but like those among men who live by sharping & robbing he is generally poor and often very lousy. Besides he is a rank coward: The little King Bird not bigger than a Sparrow attacks him boldly and drives him out of the district. He is therefore by no means a proper emblem for the brave and honest..."
>
> - Benjamin Franklin[1]

This is not to take anything away from the bird of prey, which is an integral part of numerous ecosystems and plays an important role in regulating fish populations and distributing nutrients from lakes and rivers to the forests. It's about how the as-yet-unacknowledged mythos of the bald eagle is driving our nation's culture and economy. It's about the symbolic nature of dominating others, using our sharp elbows and leveraging every advantage to improve our circumstances, while minimizing our responsibility, expense, connection, and risk.

> **WARNING:** This section is another course of bitter medicine.

The eagle is a symbol chosen by many nations (e.g., Rome, Iraq, Russia, Poland, Syria, Mexico, the Czech Republic). The Nazis were also big fans. This eagle mythos underpinned Roman law, the Doctrine of Discovery, and Calvinism, all of which crossed the ocean to the "New World." It is the unspoken purpose of the Mayflower Compact and the Massachusetts Bay Colony, establishing white settler colonialists as God's chosen and divine ones, whose "manifest destiny" was to convert, subjugate, and/or kill all others.

The myth of the eagle informed our approach towards First Nations people who we regarded as a foreign enemy, the devil, dark, lusty, lazy, and sinful. As punishment for their inconvenient existence, the Massachusetts, Connecticut, and Virginia colonies began a state-sanctioned, privatized, and total war, by providing incentives to white settlers to burn Native villages and feed stores, and receive bounties in return for the scalps taken from Native men, women, and children.

These first settler colonialists did not come over from Europe on the heels of an abundant, healthy, soulful, and connected upbringing, but rather after having been oppressed, dehumanized, and exploited for centuries by eagle doctrines in their home countries. It is no wonder that the cross, crown, reason, and Golden Rule were extended only to other white Christians, and even then, selectively. The gun and hatchet were for everyone else, especially if they had something we wanted.

As we explored, the eagle myth shaped our colonial expansion, our slavery-based economy, our relationships to one another at home, and our foreign policy. It also turned its talons upon Christianity itself. In the early 1900s, via the "Second Great Awakening," Christianity morphed into an evangelical individualism[2]. It was no longer about God's chosen white people seeking refuge in white Jesus and the white community, it was now every white person for themselves. Ministers like Charles Finney and Oral Roberts put the path to wealth and divinity in our hands, laying the foundation for the "prosperity gospel" in Reverend Ike's "Fake it 'til you make it" in black communities and Pat Robertson's televangelism in white communities. While paying lip service to divine providence, this "gospel" focused on the individual and the individual alone as the source of all good and bad fortune. It equated wealth with divinity and poverty with sin.

The eagle myth is also at the heart of our nation's booming secular religions: free market fundamentalism, consumerism, and self-improvement. To complete our transition from forager, farmer, smith, community member, and citizen to interchangeable labor input and consumer segment, we began a worship of the market's "invisible hands." We lapped up sermons from the free market fundamentalist clergy like Milton Friedman, Ayn Rand, Ronald Reagan, and Friedrich Hayek, who grounded us in the moral license to dehumanize and exploit each other with increasingly abstract economic schemes.

Over time, we built an economic ministry of control, dominance, and "red tape", where roughly one-half of the jobs and job responsibilities in our economy are what David Graeber's book *Bullshit Jobs*, suggests are *bullshit*; these are jobs that have no economic or societal benefit, could disappear without anyone noticing, and are frequently physically, morally, psychologically, and spiritually damaging. These *bullshit* jobs and responsibilities empower us to dehumanize and control each other with bureaucracy, duct tape over our systemic failures, and elevate the image and prestige of those with slightly more status and power[3].

We also created new *bullshit* products. We employed Edwin Bernays, Sigmund Freud's nephew, to help fools and their money part. Bernays translated the psychology of his uncle into irresistible subconscious advertising to manufacture the desire to fill our otherwise empty lives with goods and services that provide no discernible benefit[4]. Legions of Mad Men followed him, convincing us that wealth, land, a big home, and the latest of everything were needed for us to survive, stand out, and have worth.

According to this gospel of prosperity, markets, self-improvement gurus like Norman Vincent Peale, Werner Erhart, Tony Robbins, and Oprah Winfrey, and the Mad Men who dressed us for the occasion, we now had only one person to thank for anything good in our lives and only one to blame for anything bad: ourselves. If we didn't embody wealth, health, beauty, prestige, and boundless optimism, then it was presumed we had succumbed to the devil / limiting beliefs / loserdom.

The results are that we've become insecure and self-centered, plagued by what the Cree Nation refers to as *wetiko*, an aggressive and parasitic selfishness. A study examining the evolution of language in the United States throughout the 1900s revealed that words such as "thankfulness," "kindness," "appreciation," and "helpfulness" decreased by 56%[5]. Additionally, the average 2009 college student scored higher in narcissism on the Narcissistic Personality Inventory than 65% of students in 1982[6]; and 75% of college students in 2009 scored lower in empathy than the average student in 1979[7].

Now, empowerment and achievement are not bad things at all. In a cohesive, intact, and just society, they are a great source of self-expression, individuation, actualization, and community wealth. However, empowerment and achievement in an eagle society (one increasingly devoid of social ties, moral instincts, ecological responsibility, and shared purpose) go wrong very quickly (e.g., our two unhealed genocides, oligarchy, apartheid, subsistence wages, climate change, rape culture, etc.).

One of the main problems of the eagle mythos is the likelihood that it will actually bear any fruit. Although the media glamorizes the centralization of wealth, as marked by the meteoric rise of GDP, the Dow, and the S&P 500, and the eagles who amass gigantic fortunes (e.g., Warren Buffet, Elon Musk, and Jeff Bezos), it rarely questions why life is getting worse by the day. As we explored in the last chapter, we've transferred $50T from the bottom 90% to the top 1%, making it incredibly difficult for regular people to invest in themselves, their families, and their communities. For those of us who try to escape this scheme and become eagles ourselves by starting businesses, we must not only take a huge hit in pay, but go out of pocket for healthcare. And what is our reward for this sacrifice? 50% of us fail in our first five years and 70% fail by year 10[8].

Because we praise wealth and shame poverty, we blame the poor for their *obvious* lack of intelligence, creativity, and hard work; and when it is us on the ropes, we delude ourselves into thinking that with more hard work, soon our ship will come in. Or we turn to get-rich-quick schemes like house flipping, cryptocurrency, MLM's, or crime, or we give up all together and seek refuge in alcohol, drugs, video games, or conspiracy theories.

As John Steinbeck once mused about why the labor movement had so much trouble gaining steam in the United States, "...we didn't have any self-admitted proletarians. Everyone was a temporarily embarrassed capitalist."[9] We don't need government handouts or solidarity with other oppressed peoples, we need more hard work and a little luck to acquire enough wealth to insulate ourselves from the market morality of the eagle.

As we have explored, the suburbs contain a disproportionately white managerial class of people who own homes. They employ largely BIPOC working class people, who predominantly pay rent in the cities and exurbs to largely white owners of rental properties. Those who live in the suburbs then commute to the cities, where they make their income and enjoy entertainment, but generally do not pay any income or property tax.

The result is that suburbs have become eagles' nests, with well-maintained roads, well-funded schools and social services, smoothies, sushi, spas, gardeners, golf courses, and yoga studios. Starved of tax revenue, the exurbs and cities are marked by poverty, potholes, underfunded schools, food deserts, malnutrition, addiction, and obesity. Because the eagle's bootstraps / prosperity gospel has saturated every institution with which the poor engage (business, entertainment, religion, education), the necessary solidarity and political will required to change this arrangement never manifests.

From scalps to slavery to sharecropping to Jim Crow to lynching to gated suburbs to congested freeways to flat wages to contract lending to Hoover's Counter Intelligence Program (COINTELPRO) to harass and assassinate civil rights and labor leaders to pesticides to consumerism to forcing the Global South (broadly, the regions of Latin America, Asia, Africa, and Oceania) to take on expensive debt from the IMF and World Bank to housing projects to toxic waste dumps to poisoned air and water to privatized healthcare to union busting to rape culture to CIA coups—it's almost as if hurt people can't do anything else but devise new ways to make a buck by exploiting others. *Eagles gonna eagle.*

There are so many wonderful things to celebrate about our country, from our democratic institutions to music to crafts to technology to universities to arts to national parks to scientific achievements. However, these things exist in large part because we have taken from, oppressed, and exterminated others—nearly exclusively without remorse or repair. In the same way the gilded palace halls of Buckingham and Versailles are truly extraordinary—and yet also dirty with the blood of murder, slavery, torture, rape, and oppression—much of what is good, true, and beautiful in our society was built on the backs of those who we enslaved, oppressed, and exterminated.

Knowing the truth about our history would not bother us if we took pride in being a bunch of shifty eagles. These truths only bother us because deep down we know we *are* not. We know we are better than the murdering, thieving, raping, and enslaving of our ancestors. If we didn't hold ourselves to a higher standard, if we didn't have a powerful national purpose, reading this would produce no resistance, no knot in the pit of our stomachs.

If this makes you feel badly about our country, you are not alone. When I started to engage with this history, I was enraged. Two business degrees and $200k in student loans, for what? To build myself a life raft while everything I hold sacred drowns? Feeling sadness, shame, and anger is not bad; it's natural in the face of being miseducated and betrayed. It's healthy to feel remorse, anger, and shame when we acknowledge that we and our ancestors have been complicit in hurting others. Let us remember the suffering our ancestors caused, the danger of perpetuating it through inaction, and the redemption and renewal available to us through reckoning, responsibility, and repair.

Let us use this moment to guide us back into our ideals and purpose. Let us end our toxic relationship with the eagle, complete this chapter of U.S. history, and start a new one.

R.I.P. Eagle

(27 BCE - 2022 CE)

SORBET: With these hard truths out of the way, I again invite you to cleanse your palette. Do what you need to do to "shake it off." Perhaps a walk around the block, a good cry, or a hug might serve you.

Let us now articulate a new era of collective flourishing, healing, belonging, and purpose—one that calls forth our moral instincts and most cherished ideals, one that effectuates Dr. King's dream of "beloved community." What myth might call us into our nation's powerful purpose?

In a time when culture and politics have devolved into gang warfare, where even our flag and colors are polarizing[10], our country needs a new unifying myth to guide us into a future of collective flourishing. As the Fates would have it, this symbol arrived under auspicious skies and with bipartisan support.

"We recognize the bison as a symbol of strength and unity."

—Fred DuBray, Cheyenne River Sioux

In 2016, as a result of a bipartisan coalition in the House and Senate along with the InterTribal Buffalo Council and the National Bison Association, the bison became our national mammal—but it is much more than that. It is a symbol of strength, redemption, protection, resilience, care, courage, and our commonwealth.

From the National Park Service:

"After four years of outreach to Congress and the White House, by the Wildlife Conservation Society, its partners the InterTribal Buffalo Council and National Bison Association and 60-plus Vote Bison Coalition members, the National Bison Legacy Act was signed on May 9, 2016, officially making the bison our national mammal. This historic event represents a true comeback story, embedded with history, culture, and conservation.

To honor such an iconic and resilient species, Congress passed the National Bison Legacy Act on April 28, 2016, making the bison a U.S. symbol of unity, resilience and healthy landscapes and communities. The Act recognizes the historical, cultural, and economic importance of bison. More than 60 American Indian tribes participate in the Intertribal Buffalo Council, an organization working to help coordinate and assist tribes in returning bison back to tribal lands. Also, over one million acres of tribal land contribute to the conservation and cultural efforts of bison. Not only do bison play an important cultural role, but they also have significant economic value. Private bison producers own about 360,000 bison, creating jobs and providing a healthy meat source as well as leather and wool products to the American public. Bison also play an important ecological role, beneficially influencing prairie ecosystems through their grazing patterns and behavior.

Although the recognition does not convey new protections for the bison, the Act recognizes the great conservation success story and importance of its comeback to Native Americans and rural communities alike. This new and permanent designation conveys a vision of shared values of unity, resilience and healthy landscapes and communities. No other species is so iconic of American history and culture like the bison."[11]

The Bison Way

The myth of the bison elicits something deep in our souls. It connects us to rolling prairies, lush forests, rushing rivers, majestic peaks, the rising sun, a prismatic dusk, and a starry sky. It calls us into individual and collective power. It calls us into relationship with wild nature, play, community, and adventure. It beckons us to be grateful for natural beauty, and summons us to care for all that is sacred. It also comes with its own operating system, a new set of national ethics far different than those of the bald eagle:

- **COURAGE** - Unlike cattle, bison run straight into an approaching storm to move through it quickly—an apt metaphor for the hard truths we must face as a nation and the necessary reforms we must implement to address polarization, racial justice, rape culture, climate change, and income inequality.
- **CARE** - Bison care for the most vulnerable by placing them in the center of the herd—an equally apt metaphor for the way we must holistically care for our sick, depressed, traumatized, young, elderly, disabled, and historically marginalized.
- **INCLUSION** - Bison make room for other species to graze, drink, and play, sharing close space with elk, moose, deer, and winged ones—another metaphor for the diverse relationships we are summoned to develop in our economy, communities, ecologies, and foreign policy.
- **PLAY** - Bison spend a good deal of time at play with each other, laying about, nudging each other, or running off together.
- **INDEPENDENCE** - Bison make room for themselves. Although they move about as herds, they can often be found wandering alone, as if solitude, leisure, and discovery were all that mattered.
- **GENERATIVITY** - Through their play, wallowing, and grazing, bison till the soil, protect fresh water springs, and play a vital role in the ecological resilience of their habitats, cultivating the

diversity of plant, insect, and bird populations. Bison are a symbol of genuine prosperity for many First Nations, a symbol of "give-away," of purpose, of contributing their "100 gifts" towards the betterment of all.

- **PROTECTION** - Bison are ornery if provoked. They are fiercely protective of themselves and their community, leveraging their incredible strength, acceleration and speed (up to 40 mph) to ward off threats, and gore if necessary. Another apt metaphor for the spirit we must bring to tending to the social, emotional, and environmental health of our people and communities, as well as the power and responsibility organizations have to protect and heal our nation.

- **REDEMPTION** - To clear the west for farming and railroads, the bison were nearly exterminated. Because of their majesty— their aesthetic and moral value— and the critical role they play in many ecosystems, we have chosen to bring them back, to make room for them to thrive, and allow them to guide us into a deeper expression of who we are.

So, what does this mean for us? It means that we can allow the mythos of the bison to work on us individually—to move through us and into greater courage, care, inclusion, play, independence, protection, generativity, and redemption. This set of ethics is neither liberal nor conservative, but rather evokes the fullest expression of both attitudes. Within these ethics, we find greater compassion and power, greater equity and individual achievement, greater connection and courage.

It means we remember who we are deep down, who we once were as children, foragers and simple farmers, before the eagle broke us, forced us to work ourselves to the bone, turn on each other, and surrender our hearts, bodies, mutual concern, rituals, coherent cosmologies, rich languages, and inspired ethics. This doesn't mean abdicating our will or purpose—what makes us unique—or necessitate that we become pagans or socialists, but rather, remembering that, as we bring forth our gifts, we acknowledge that we, too, are mammals who are fundamentally intuitive, relational, and responsive. We are of, by, and for the earth and each other.

It means we remember that we're imbued with voice, emotions, and neurochemicals that bind us to one another[12]. We have evolved with empathy and altruism—not pure selfishness—to survive. We are wired to care, connect, feel, communicate, play, relate, and cooperate[13].

As we begin the Era of the Bison, we cannot simply say "the past is the past," wipe the slate clean, and begin anew. That has never worked. People carry the wounds and injustices of the past into the present, via their neighborhoods, epigenetic expressions of trauma[14], oral histories, dysfunctional family dynamics, cemeteries, unmarked and mass graves, and the eagle's institutional norms that still perpetuate harm. Reckoning and repair are required if we are to be redeemed and renewed.

"The past is never dead. It's not even past."

- William Faulkner

It's time to accept that we are all in recovery, in a post-traumatic response to centuries of dehumanization and oppression extending back to at least the Roman Empire. What many of us consider to be our personalities, careers, and culture are really coping mechanisms we've developed to endure centuries of trauma in order to survive. As a result, we're all in varying stages of grief, healing, and recovery. To heal from our multiple traumas and enter a period of post-traumatic growth, we must turn towards one another as bison do, and as we did during the Abolition, Labor, Suffrage and Civil Rights Movements, to sing, grieve, lament, heal, create, and rejoice.

So, what does this mean for you as a leader? It means we must guide our organizations towards greater connection to, and care for, the commonwealth. It means we must view the world and each business decision through the lens of resilience and long-term wealth of the bison, versus extraction and short-term profits of the eagle.

It means we must also be vigilant for the remnants of the eagle mythos still preying on our thinking, marriages, families, and neighborhoods, as we develop new ways to communicate, connect, lead, and do business.

To do so means we transform our approach to our people, culture, and learning. We no longer view people as an expense to be reduced, but rather as a source of long-term wealth, resilience, and innovation. It means we move labor from a line item expense on the income statement—from something to be minimized in service of shareholder profit—to an asset on our balance sheets—something to be invested in, cultivated, and protected. We no longer abdicate our responsibility for culture and well-being, but intentionally develop it. It means that we view each person as whole: with emotions, a soul, trauma, a life outside of work, family responsibilities, and a community. All of these need tending.

It means we see each person as worthy of dignity and prosperity, that we bless the beauty of each soul, empower each person to develop a connection to their purpose, and the opportunity to shape their lives and careers in its image. It means that we find our unique connection to our organization's mission and values. It means we take a stand on the pressing issues in our society and environment and err on the side of making mistakes in service of the bison ethos.

It means we are bold, vocal, and hold ourselves accountable to our purpose values by treating each other with dignity as B Corps do and having fun. As the Maine Beer Company articulates by following its purpose, "Do the right thing":

"Maine Beer Company strives to hire a talented, thoughtful and diverse workforce that contributes to the overall culture of the company... Maine Beer Company offers all full-time employees 100% employer-paid health insurance, at least three weeks paid time off, paid holidays, 401k Safe Harbor contributions and profit sharing, referral bonuses, dental insurance, parental leave, and Employee Assistance Programs. And, don't forget about the free beer![15]"

It means we are deliberately developmental—seeking to unlock and activate human potential within and outside of our organizations. It means we bring care to each phase of the employee lifecycle, from candidate to new hire to leader to alumni.

It means we stop applying the eagle's paternalistic approach to people, where we view them as selfish actors who need to be reformed, assimilated, and motivated with compliance, incentives, and punishments. It means we move from a talent ethos of "culture fit" towards celebrating our uniqueness as a "culture add." It means we adopt an ethos of healing, empowerment, and connection, bringing people together to learn about themselves and each other in a safe and effective way. It means we end our reliance on one-time compliance trainings, and build a culture through ongoing and immersive social learning experiences, where learning and authentic connection are part of the normal course of business. It means we stop our extractive and oppressive business practices and look to regenerative, cradle-to-cradle approaches to meet customer needs.

This might sound nice and all, but at least some part of you might be thinking that if you tell your investors or board that you're doing this, they'll fire you on the spot. You'll ruin your reputation, lose your house, and hurt your family. Luckily, you have more than the people, history, your moral instincts, and the iconic archetype of the bison on your side. You also have powerful data to build buy-in.

It is perhaps a great irony that there is a more compelling business case for activating bison ethics than the extractive status quo of the eagle. But, it is so. Applying the bison ethos and activating purpose and belonging, you can expect to realize more than $20k per employee per year in additional productivity and an additional 7.4 months in average tenure[16,17]. Given that the average tenure of an employee is about 4 years, that's an expected gain of $80k+ per employee. Let's say you hire coaches for each of your employees at $6,000/year—that's a 3.3x return. Let's say you activate purpose and belonging with small, diverse, peer-learning groups at $500/year for each of your employees—that's a 40x return.

This is obviously not an iterative improvement, but rather a step-function change in collective flourishing. It's the realization of Heather McGhee's "solidarity dividend." Additionally, productivity and tenure aren't all you'll improve by activating purpose and belonging. If you decide to take this path, it will benefit all of your key stakeholders: your investors, customers, and employees:

Investors

- Stakeholder-driven companies outperform S&P 500 by 100%[18].
- Purpose-driven companies posted a 9.85% CAGR, versus 2.4% for the S&P Consumer Sector[19].
- Purpose-driven companies outperform their peers by 12:1[20].

Customers
- Global consumers are 4-6x more likely to trust, buy from, champion, and protect companies that lead with purpose[21].
- 6 of every 10 consumers, and 9 of 10 millennials, say they will buy from a company that leads with purpose[22].

- 87% of global consumers believe businesses should put at least as much emphasis on social interests as business ones[23].
- Gen-Z consumers are 85% more likely to trust a brand, 84% more likely to buy their products, and 82% more likely to recommend that brand to their friends and family if a brand supports a cause[24].
- 6 of every 10 Americans would choose, switch, avoid, or boycott a brand based on its stand on societal issues, compared to 5 of 10 in 2017[25].

Employee Productivity, Engagement, and Satisfaction
- Purpose-driven employees are 175% more productive[26].
- Purpose is correlated with a 333% increase in organizational commitment[27].
- 90% of global employees in purpose-driven companies are engaged[28] versus 20% of the global workforce who are engaged[29].
- Purpose-driven leaders have employees who are 70% more satisfied, 56% more engaged, and 100% more likely to stay at your organization[30].

By activating the myth of bison, we deliver for our employees, customers, communities, shareholders, nation, and ecosystems. We also engage in a new covenant and a shared identity that helps redeem the sins of our ancestors, putting meat on the bones of "life, liberty, and the pursuit of happiness" for all, and transmuting *pluribus* into *unum*.

In the next chapter, "Culture Change is a Matter of Life and Death," we explore what is at stake in activating this shift towards the bison.

Chapter 2 Summary:

- Every nation has a myth that governs their actions towards each other, the earth, and other nations. The same is true for organizations.
- We have been shaped by the myth of the eagle, a parasitic individualism that has resulted in slavery, genocide, an apartheid, climate change, rape culture, and a $50T wealth transfer to the 1%.
- We have an opportunity to adopt a new myth—the way of the bison—to reckon with our past, accept responsibility, repair the damage caused, and be redeemed and renewed.
- By most measures, bison-led companies significantly outperform those that do not.

Chapter 2 Reflection Questions:

- Where in your life are you guided by the eagle? (health, romance, family, work, community, home location, finances, spirituality)
- Where in your life do you feel the ethics of the bison present? (health, romance, family, work, community, home location, finances, spirituality)
- What would it be like to work in your organization if it was guided by the bison?
- What would your community be like if the 20 largest employers in your area were guided by the bison?

Chapter 3

Culture is a Matter of Life and Death

"Maybe that works for y'all out in California, but we're sitting on a powder keg right now."

I was talking with a friend of mine who is the head of DEI of a 300,000+ person global technology company.

"How do you mean?" I inquired.

"We've got All Lives Matter MAGA folks here. Good people who do a great job, but who create this constant hostility and resistance to anything DEI. We can't put them in a training with people of color. It'll re-traumatize folks. They'll leave, I'll miss my DEI targets, and then I'll have to leave. I'm already seeing disproportionately high early retirements and leaves of absence for women and people of color. If we start a big culture change effort, I think it will only get worse."

And, she was right. It was July of 2020, just weeks after George Floyd's murder, and the media's "divide and conquer" approach had reached a fever pitch, pitting conservatives against liberals, cities against suburbs, and All Lives Matter against Black Lives Matter. She knew she had to do something beyond providing mental health resources and public statements, and that even a public statement was going to kick the hornets' nest.

As we've explored, this dynamic exists because traditional DEI approaches, such as unconscious bias trainings, anti-discrimination trainings, anonymous reporting systems, employee resource groups (ERGs), and hiring quotas, frequently have a shaming, corrective, and paternalistic feel. It is no surprise that many white folks consciously resist or tune it out, and subconsciously deepen the sense of feeling attacked and the need to protect their identity and way of life. As we previously learned, the result is that the DEI industry as a whole has failed to deliver positive outcomes in hiring, retention, and promotion of diverse candidates over the last two decades.

Given this history, introducing new or expanded DEI efforts at any time is a giant risk. In the wake of multiple videos documenting the murders of BIPOC folks by police, a summer of protests, and one of the most consequential elections in U.S. history, that risk expanded 10 times.

It also seems that our attitude towards racial justice is rooted in our partisan identity. For example, 85% among folks who lean left support BLM, and 78% of those who lean right oppose it[1]. Similarly, 91% of Democrats say black people face a lot of discrimination in our society versus 42% of Republicans[2]. This suggests that the topics of diversity, race, equity, and inclusion are likely to ignite these deeper racial/partisan identities and further aggravate the situation. My friend was right: DEI is indeed risky business.

While some white folks opened their hearts and began the journey to allyship in 2020, some dug their heels in deeper. What's abundantly clear is that we cannot keep doing the same things and expect different results.

Death to the Tyrants!

Unfortunately, our political / racial tribalism isn't merely one of catty clicks and scornful frowns. Many believe that the other side should suffer and die. 54% of us believe our fellow citizens are the biggest threat to our country[3]. 33% of us now justify the use of violence for political gains[4], with 15% of Democrats and 20% of Republicans believing it would be a good thing if a bunch of folks on the other side just died[5].

If folks are in the 33% of us who support violence, and they feel culture, race, and/or politics play a role in them being passed over for promotion or in their dismissal, then it could get very bad, very quickly. (Of course, this threat wouldn't be such an issue if AR-15's and ammonium nitrate were not so easily accessible.) Obviously, we talking about much more than a business risk. It's more than people not getting along, not trusting each other, or not wanting to collaborate with or promote diverse colleagues. This is a deep tear in the moral fabric of society and it impacts our bodies, minds, souls, and democratic institutions. I am not crying wolf; the threat is as real as the chair you're sitting in. I know this from personal experience.

In the summer of 2020, my wife and I painted our windows and put up a Black Lives Matter sign in our yard to show our support for the BIPOC folks in our community. After a few weeks, our sign was defaced, so we fixed it. Shortly thereafter, a neighbor alerted me that our house had been targeted. Someone who lived a couple miles away had taken a photo of our home and posted it along with our address on the Instagram feed @DarkNightSD. This person was holding public discussions about bringing death to the tyrants (BLM supporters) and forming a militia to take us out, along with the other homes in our area voicing support for BLM. Let me repeat: he wanted to *take us OUT.*

I reported it to the San Diego Police Department along with proof of @DarkNightSD's link to the personal account of this person. After I told the dispatcher what had happened, and described the evidence I had in my phone, she said, "So, what did these Black Lives Matter people do to you again?" I was shocked. Had she not heard anything I said? How could she think this person's white supremacist actions had anything do with Black Lives Matter supporters?

Three hours later, two units showed up and I told them what had happened. I offered to show them the evidence in my phone and they declined to look at it. Instead they invited me to take down the signs. They told me there is violence and intimidation on both sides of the issue. Both sides of what, I wondered? Then it clicked for me why the dispatcher thought it was BLM supporters who were suspected. It was clear that SDPD viewed BLM negatively, and it was likely that their "news" sources were the same ones painting BLM as a domestic terror organization—which is literally the opposite of what it is. BLM is an organization to mobilize support for stopping the terror rendered upon communities of color by police and white nationalists[6].

A friend advised me to report the incident to the FBI, which I did, but heard nothing. Another friend at the Department of Justice talked to her colleague who tracked domestic terrorism incidents. Her colleague did this covertly, of course, as the Trump administration officially ignored it and allocated no resources to stopping it[7]. I learned that politically and racially motivated domestic terror incidents were popping up all over the country: spraying blue dots on the curbs of Biden supporters in Roseville, California[8], the lynchings in Palmdale, California[9], and hanging nooses in Connecticut[10]. She also told me that nothing was going to happen about it unless there was a change in the DOJ's policy on domestic terrorism.

And, as surveys reveal, many of us likely have family and friends inclined towards the use of violence, even if they've never said anything about it to us. We also are clear that this is the beginning of something far worse. 51% of us expect an increase in violence[11], 71% of us believe democracy itself is in jeopardy[12], and 93% of us recognize that our hatred for each other is a problem[13]. This problem is pervasive—and a change is needed.

Given the January 6th denialism, defensiveness, and obstructionism, the deep divisions in Congress, and the recent perversions of electoral integrity across the majority of states, we are in what Robert Kagan of the Brookings Institute called "a constitutional crisis"[14], with violence likely in 2024, if not sooner. Put another way, we are in what Boston University professor and former Reagan administration State Department Official, Angelo Codevilla, termed a "cold civil war." Despite no evidence of election fraud, 82% of Fox viewers and 97% of OAN viewers[15] believe President Biden was not justly elected, with one publicly asking, "When do we get to use the guns?"[16]

We need only recall the 1994 Rwandan genocide to see how quickly things can escalate from cold to hot, from disinformation and hate speech to genocide and war. There were months and months of vitriol on the radio, while tens of thousands of machetes were quietly distributed. Then the long waited-for cue—"Kill the cockroaches"—came over the radio. Within the next 100 days, 500,000 to 1,100,000 Rwandans were dead.

Of course it can be argued that the conditions in Rwanda aren't exactly the same as those in our nation today. But, they aren't that different either. It wasn't that long ago that our nation tore itself apart over our differing views on who deserves life, liberty, and the pursuit of happiness. 750,000 of us died in the Civil War, representing 2.5% of the population. If 2.5% of our nation died today, that would be 7,000,000 deaths. It wasn't that long ago that Germany tore the world in two for strikingly similar reasons.

Was January 6th a dry run for a civil war, like Hitler's 1923 failed coup? It is hard to say, but with easily available ammonium nitrate, 46% of us owning 393,000,000 guns[17], and 33% of us in support of political violence, the stakes and risks have never been higher. It goes without saying that our lives, careers and communities depend on peace and a working democracy.

Further, this hate and risk of violence doesn't operate outside of our economy. It's not a hobby or a side hustle. It is deeply enmeshed in our culture at large, including the economy. It's in the hearts of our investors, employees, and customers. With over 10,000,000 U.S. citizens sympathizing with the insurrection and white nationalism[18], we now have 838 registered white supremacist hate groups in the United States, nearly an all-time high[19]. But you might never know if your neighbors, customers, employees, and investors are white nationalists, as 63% of us are afraid to share our political views, and almost a third of us self-censor our political beliefs for fear of losing our jobs[20].

These are the people representing your brand, holding your shares, servicing your customers, trying to collaborate together on teams, and buying your products. As you might imagine, these attitudes fuel further divisive rhetoric, and have significant economic consequences. According to a faculty report from Harvard Business School, political dysfunction is the #1 barrier to strengthening our nation's economic competitiveness[21].

In the wake of these deep divisions and increasingly violent tribalism, it's clear that our approaches to culture, including DEI, must be completely re-envisioned. We must build connections and cultivate shared purpose, lower the temperature and elevate our common humanity. Like everything else pre-pandemic, pre-George Floyd's murder, and pre-January 6, we must bring greater care and intention to how we shape culture.

When even the words "diversity," "equity," and "inclusion" raise hairs on the backs of many white necks, we must address inequity and racism with more than a traditional DEI approach. We can't keep punching white folks on the nose with it; it just doesn't work. It likely never did. We have to treat the problem holistically and systematically. To do so, we must root out the eagle in all its forms and cultivate the bison.

How We Can Heal

Our last chance against this deluge of danger, despair, disarray, dehumanization, and democratic collapse is the organization. Work is now how many people get the majority of their needs met: income, healthcare, meaning, connection, growth, and achievement. It is the plow, ale house, church, school, and hospital rolled up into one. While I think most of us would want it to be otherwise—having a fulfilling career, with affordable quality healthcare disentangled from work, and a shorter and flexible work week with time for friends, family, the outdoors, religion, and civic engagement—work is still the centerpiece of our nation's culture and identity.

As such, work is the root of all that is good and bad about our nation. Which is also to say that organizational leaders are responsible for what continues to be good and bad about it. And, with the clarity about what we know to be missing—purpose, belonging, connection, and common cause—we have an incredible opportunity to take responsibility for leading our nation into the bison era and establishing a meaningful legacy.

As leaders, in times of peace, we have to be grounded in our purpose and values, look at the data dispassionately, assess the risks and opportunities, and invest our time and resources wisely. In times of crisis, we must not only take wise and purposeful action to heal, but also substantial, systemic, and sustained action to prevent further harm. *This is a time of multiple crises:* we are unwell, impoverished, sad, angry, disempowered, and heavily armed.

As my friend, Renée Smith, the CEO of A Human Workplace[22], observed: "This is our Apollo 13 moment." She was referencing a scene from the movie, *Apollo 13*, when Mission Control realizes that the astronauts will not survive unless they rebuild the ship's CO_2 filter mid-flight.

This is what needs to be done now. We must realize that our flight plans from 2019—and even those from 2020, 2021, and 2022—are useless. We have to turn all our cards face up and start playing a new game. We must soberly embrace the current reality: Organizations are currently a nesting ground for hate, divisiveness, *bullshit* roles and responsibilities, burnout and mental health epidemics, and business models that are responsible for the vast majority of greenhouse gasses[23]. Our supply chains are vulnerable, our democratic institutions are crumbling, our employees want living wages, purpose and belonging, extreme weather is decimating our communities, and customers want purpose-driven, carbon-neutral products.

It's time to rethink everything with the bison ethos in mind and heart. It's time to place all of our tools, our purpose, our values, and our people functions on the table to rebuild our cultures and businesses from the ground up.

Before we dive into how to transform our organizations, let's look at how the various ways the eagle and bison show up and manifest at work.

Chapter 3 Summary:

- The eagle has divided us against each other along the lines of ideology and race, and it's eroding the foundations of our organizations, society, economy, and democracy.
- The use of violence is supported by 1/3 of us, expected by most of us, and regarded as a problem by almost all of us.
- Organizations cannot keep developing people and culture in the same ways; they are not working.
- Organizations must scrap all their plans, dump everything on the table, and rebuild their businesses and cultures mid-flight with an entirely new ethos.

Chapter 3 Reflection Questions:

- Where do you see the impacts of racial animosity and political tribalism in your life?
- How do they impact your organization?
- Have you ever felt that we'd be better off without those with whom you disagree?
- What will you do in the face of our *Apollo 13* moment?

Chapter 4

Bison @Work

"White guys won't work here anymore."

"Wait, what? What do you mean?" I said to a friend of mine who heads talent for a multinational technology company. I was shocked to hear that, as her company had a great reputation.

"This month, I had two white guys from Texas turn down great offers because the company wasn't diverse enough. I never thought I'd see the day when white guys are saying they need women and people of color on their teams."

"Holy cow! I just got chills," I exclaimed.

"I've been harping on this for years," she replied. "I've been telling our CHRO that the time would come when we've fallen too far behind in creating a place that attracts diverse talent."

That time has obviously come. Because of the racial tensions in society that we explored in the last chapter, 90% of white male workers currently place some value on DEI, with 42% who believe it is very or extremely important to them. Additionally, 55% of all employees (and 45% of white employees) believe that racism at work has damaged their relationship with their employer[1]. Now, 4 in 10 white employees avoid employers who don't take a stand against racism[2]—far exceeding the 25% tipping point threshold required for a belief or behavior to penetrate an entire population. While racial and political tribalism in broader society are on the rise, it appears that there is something hopeful happening inside of organizations. It appears that many are ready for a change, but the eagle's norms, institutions and cultures haven't yet evolved to meet this new paradigm.

This gives me hope. If there is any silver lining to the 2020 summer of protests, it is that we shook the tree of liberty, and a bunch of aspiring white allies fell out to defend it.

That certainly happened to me and Mike, my conservative CEO friend. We were part of 2020's bumper harvest of white folks committed to change. Many of us deepened our learning, reading *White Fragility* and *How to Be an Antiracist*, formed book clubs, joined ERGs, took inclusion trainings, joined our local SURJ Chapter (Showing Up for Racial Justice), donated to organizations like Black Lives Matter (BLM), National Association for the Advancement of Colored Peoples (NAACP), and the Equal Justice Initiative (EJI), and took to the streets alongside our BIPOC friends and family. Public support for Black Lives Matter increased to 55% by September of 2020, up from 43% in 2016[4]. Corporations followed suit announcing over 100,000 new DEI roles, issuing bold statements and initiatives, and pledging $50 billion to see it through. However, due to white backlash, disinformation, and other pandemic-related priorities, their progress has stalled[5].

So, what is an organization to do? Traditionally, DEI meant recruiting at historically black colleges and universities (HBCUs), providing mentorship, forming ERG's, and paying living wages. Today, these are simply table stakes. In light of our cascading crises, today's workers want to be a part of something that matters. They want to join a mission they can easily find on Maslow's Needs Hierarchy or the UN's Sustainable Development Goals, and to be a part of a team where everyone belongs and everyone is supported to do their best work.

Of course, these have always been concerns of women and people from the LGBTQIA+ and BIPOC communities. Now, it matters to almost all of us, especially younger folks. If the culture of a business stinks, which we can easily tell from listening to industry gossip, reading the company's website, and checking out Glassdoor ratings, we'll keep looking.

Companies have tried to fix the symptoms of their brokens cultures with lame proclamations ginned up by consultants and marketing teams. They've tried individual interventions like games, apps, free food, mentorship, and volunteering opportunities. Ultimately, these tactical point solutions failed to produce substantial and sustained results because they sat on top of the eagle's nest of divisive, dysfunctional, and dehumanizing business practices. With the eagle's underlying biases (privileging whites and men) and cultural norms (always on, impress the boss, similarity bias), and systems (profit principle/quarterly earning reports, performance reviews, quotas), individual interventions don't stand a chance.

We are experiencing a whole system failure, but few companies recognize it. Most companies still think that more individual interventions are the answer. We can't "ice cream social" our way out of a toxic culture. We can't app our way out of long hours. We can't pill our way out of a crappy boss. We can't hire our way out of employee burnout and turnover. We can't blog our way out of racism. We can't deck chair our way out of a hull breach.

We need to think holistically about the problem. It's time for a new way.

To do this we must remember that like the bison, we are a herd species. We exist by, for, and through each other. We need each other, and we always have. The neuroscience of empathy reveals that, when one of us suffers, we all suffer[6]. As such, people strategies must now be reimagined with a holistic and social approach.

A few innovative companies, such as Coursera, have begun to swing the pendulum from the eagle to the bison, revealing the increasing number of dependencies between DEI, leadership development (L+D), corporate social responsibility (CSR), wellness, talent management, and culture. They understand that each needs to be reimagined and will inform and intersect with each other[7]. For example, it is now well understood that pollution and climate change have disproportionate impacts on people of color[8], and systemic racism has been named a public health crisis[9].

Accordingly, Coursera is dissolving HR silos and is actively crafting new ways to care for the whole person and the community. Wellness initiatives are now informed by, and amplify, priorities of DEI, CSR, Talent and L+D. L+D is moving towards an inclusive/social/wellness/culture-forward pedagogy. Talent, workforce planning, policies for hiring, performance management, promotion, and compensation will include culture, DEI, and learning goals. DEI strategies will address more than biases and behavior change; they are also informing culture, learning, wellness, marketing, supply chain, and product development.

It's still too early to tell the results, but at least Coursera is asking the right questions and thinking holistically, systemically, and socially. Before we explore the particulars of what life looks like when the pendulum swings towards the bison, let's do a thorough audit to assess our starting point.

Granted, most organizations are somewhere in between the eagle and bison, it is illustrative to see where we've come from and where we're headed.

Eagle @Work

Although HR folks are, in general, incredibly thoughtful, kind, self-aware, and compassionate, the systems and cultures in which they operate are frequently individualistic, allopathic, and dehumanizing. Employees are often regarded as capital, as objects, as selfish, interchangeable children who are expected to leave everything important to them—such as their love lives, souls, families, communities, faiths, and nation—at the door. Further, the default is to consider them to be immune from the ongoing socioeconomic dynamics of the world, such as flat wages, skyrocketing housing, education, and transportation costs, police brutality, climate change, income inequality, political corruption, and systemic sexism and racism.

Eagle HR has spent the last 30 years attempting individual interventions to address the collective failures of this approach. This approach assumes that, if we're uneducated, we simply need to learn information from superior beings, e.g. experts and trainers. If we're unhappy, then a pill, program, or app will turn our frowns upside down. The assumption is that there is nothing unique about any of us—that when we come to work, we are *tabula rasa*, a blank slate, interchangeable cogs without any need for purpose and belonging.

In light of the decades of flat wages, increasing job insecurity, and the decay of society, we have a general fear of HR's power over our income, housing, and healthcare and a general insecurity about our worth and value to the company. So we hedge our bets, play "cover your ass" (CYA), put in "face time," and withhold our best ideas and dissenting opinions for fear of upsetting our superiors (in my experience, this is even more true for folks from less privileged backgrounds). When our efforts are insufficient or we miss our targets, we regard our emotions as bad, our failings as moral and personal, and ourselves as always needing to work harder, or at least maintain the appearance of working hard.

As you might imagine, this dynamic does not serve us well, and is marked by high levels of stress, burnout, disengagement, and employee turnover.

Let's take a closer look, exploring a few key HR functions:

Eagle L+D

Eagle L+D separates and treats us as individual students who learn from experts in live or virtual classrooms. We are given information and then tested on it. We pass or fail and sometimes we get a certificate or badge to put on our intranet or LinkedIn profile. Unfortunately, because we forget 90% of everything we learn within 7 days[10], and since most trainings are one-offs and outside of the flow of work, it is fair to say that a great portion of the $367B global L+D industry[11] is wasted.

Further, eagle L+D frequently allocates resources in an elitist fashion: with cheap, ineffective, and boring e-learning, of which only 3.8% is engaging[12], for frontline and low wage employees (who are typically more female and diverse). Whereas expensive training programs, off-sites, and 1:1 coaching are provided exclusively to executives and high-potential leaders (who are typically more male and white), thereby enforcing existing inequities.

Eagle DEI

Eagle DEI typically includes hiring quotas, mentoring, ERG's, anonymous reporting systems, and compliance training. It is heavy on one-time, discrimination, systemic racism, and unconscious bias training—which have been proven to be a waste of time, as most people revert to their biased behavior within 24 hours of the training[13]. This reversion happens because human moral and intuitive reasoning is rooted, not in logic, selfishness, or even altruism, but rather in the norms of our groups. We each have an internal subconscious moral calculus that has us make decisions based on the center of gravity present in our peer / family / community groups[14]. So, without changing the culture and systems, folks revert to the norm even following a breakthrough / experience / intervention.

Further, these trainings often do not meaningfully address the "just-world fallacy,"[15] the secular counterpart to "prosperity gospel," wherein people think good things happen to good people and bad things happen to bad people. The result is that—however well intended DEI programs are, and despite occasional breakthroughs—they are not enough to overcome the beliefs and norms that link success and goodness.

Another often ignored bias is the "better than average effect,"[16] wherein most of us believe we are kinder and more just than the average person, and/or that we don't have many biases compared to the average person. Research has shown that we consistently underestimate our gender and racial biases, and that those with the strongest prejudices are more likely to underestimate their biases[17].

Additionally, eagle DEI is premised on the unspoken assumption that somehow folks in the in-group (white, male, cis-gendered, heterosexuals), when delivered a training on systemic racism, will somehow just "get" what it's like to live under 400 years of a white supremacist apartheid. Somehow their hearts will magically open and new actions, structures, and equity will quickly ensue. Instead, we need to unlearn everything we've learned about U.S. history and capitalism and start over. As we explored in Chapters 1 and 2, the invention of whiteness, Manifest Destiny, the genocides, slavery, Jim Crow, and the preschool-to-prison pipeline in schools have as much to do with our culture—the lived experience of our team members and the biases they and their families must navigate on a daily basis—as their roles, responsibilities, and performance. But, re-education alone isn't enough.

To create true solidarity, we need to nurture relationships among diverse folks, share life and work experiences, work together on something that matters to all of us, understand our cultural differences, and develop new group norms. It's not about white folks "getting" the experience of BIPOC folks. That cannot ever fully happen. Solidarity is about humility, knowing we'll never fully get it—no matter how many books we read, Black folks we befriend, or museums we visit.

Solidarity occurs when we do the opposite of "divide and conquer." It requires that we connect across our differences over time, acknowledge and feel our shared humanity, and recognize we're all suffering under the eagle's norms and institutions. When we do, we embrace the value and dignity of every human life, and understand that a person's level of health and success has a great deal to do with the circumstances of their upbringing, as well as the privileges extended or denied to them. Solidarity is about acknowledgement and commitment, making a firm declaration to stand with folks who are on the receiving end of white supremacy, and committing to end it in all its forms.

But, that isn't the way of the eagle. Eagle DEI separates diverse populations into ERG's, creating insular personal networks[18] and edifing our nation's history of division, secrecy, and mistrust between groups (e.g., poor Scots-Irish elevated in status by law and encouraged to join our frontier rangers, slave patrols, strike-breaking militias, and police to harass, oppress, and kill BIPOC folks). It is also paternalistic, such as when we treat people like children who are behaving or performing poorly and separate the troublemakers:

- Diverse people need jobs, mentorship, ERGs, training, and money to become more professional, aka "act white", and
- White people need mandatory, one-time discrimination and bias trainings to magically eliminate their racist biases.

While mentoring is desired by, and impactful for, diverse candidates, it actually reduces their tenure[19]. Eagle DEI does indeed provide information and skills to people, but because it is not centered in purpose, folks don't see inclusion as an expression of their identity, but rather as something exogenous to it. It also doesn't create high-trust connections between diverse people, so it produces conscious and unconscious resistance to diverse groups and DEI initiatives as a whole.

Given all of this, it is no surprise that the $8 billion DEI spend[20] has resulted in neutral to negative outcomes over the last 2 decades and may even be making matters worse[21].

Eagle Culture

The eagle way of developing culture is not to develop culture. Instead, culture is frequently ignored and if acknowledged at all, is as an afterthought or quickly deprioritized. Sure, ice cream socials, holiday parties, volunteering, town halls, and happy hours have some benefits. They are excellent opportunities to take a break from the routine and, when done well, are great ways to recognize people's contributions and foster common purpose. However, these occasions rarely involve intentional relationship development beyond icebreakers like "two truths and a lie," treasure hunts, three-legged races, and bingo. Regardless of how well they are done, due to their infrequency, on Monday, people go back to the old paradigm.

And yet, relationships do indeed form at work and culture does indeed develop. Without being explicitly addressed and cultivated, similarity bias[22] forms around the lowest common denominators of age, race, gender, politics, and sexuality, ensuring that insular packs form. All you have to do is stand up on a chair at your next company event and observe who is talking to whom. White sales folks talking to white marketing folks. Asian engineers talking to Asian quality control folks. Black customer service reps talking to Black administrative assistants. And, those with the most power holding court in the corner with their direct reports. This results in a culture of disparate tribes resisting change and edifying existing exclusionary power dynamics[23].

Moreover, the role "office mom" is typically not part of anyone's title, so it gets assumed by, or "voluntold" to, lower status folks[24]. Typically these are white women, who add these responsibilities onto their already-packed schedules and unbalanced workloads. Without any time, staff, or budget to think it through, it gets done quickly at best, and expresses the tastes (food, music, activities) and unconscious biases of those in charge. This further edifies the dynamic that culture doesn't matter, because it's done poorly, driven by someone with relatively low status, and/or it doesn't include everyone, least of all remote workers. This dynamic is part of what causes remote workers to have 50% fewer work friends than workers in offices[25].

At its worst, this becomes an opportunity for "office moms" to flex their biases and relative power by allocating budgets for Fourth of July activities—but none for Juneteenth or Pride, for Christmas and Hanukkah activities—but none for Diwali, Eid, or Kwanza. The message is that only what is rooted in whiteness, heterosexuality, and the Judeo-Christian tradition matters.

Eagle Wellness

The ethos of eagle wellness is: "Work is hell. Eat some broccoli, exercise, take a pill, and get back to work." This is reflective of our sickcare industry, which addresses the symptoms of our atomized, poorly/micro-managed, soulless, and dehumanizing workplaces. It labels and stigmatizes mental illness, psychological languishing, and physical illness, and produces a culture of denial and victim-blaming.

It treats the crises of connection and fulfilling work as individual failures. It assumes that, if we are not healthy, happy, and productive, then we the employees are to blame. So, it doles out tips, tools, podcasts, apps, hacks, and pills to get us back on the job, but doesn't give us what we actually need to cure our burnout and languishing: fewer hours, *bullshit*-free roles, living wages, purpose, and belonging.

Research shows that individual interventions designed to increase happiness and improve mental health may actually make us more lonely[26] and unhappier[27]. In this way, eagle wellness is indistinguishable from the efforts of agricultural veterinarians, whose job is to make the animals we eat just well enough to be exploited.

As work and money are the top causes of stress[28], it should be no surprise that few turn to their abuser for comfort. Despite 97% of us being unhealthy[29], 84% of us being stressed[30], 49% of us not making a living wage[31], only 24% of us make use of wellness benefits[32]. Although a handful of great, award-winning, wellness programs exist that are part of a holistic culture of purpose, transformation, connection, balance, and health, most wellness programs face the daunting task of marshaling comparatively little time, power, and budget to combat the eagle's perfect storm of hyperindividualism, overwork, job insecurity, systemic biases, and income inequity.

The pandemic revealed and exacerbated many of the eagle's impacts. According to a June 2021 Gartner study[33]:

- 85% of us have experienced higher levels of burnout
- 41% of us have lower trust in our teams
- 40% of us report declines in our work-life balance
- 37% of us have lower trust in leadership
- 34% of us experienced a decline in psychological safety
- 31% of us report less inclusion

Of course, like nearly all dynamics in our nation, women, children, and communities of color are disproportionately impacted. Despite unemployment rates reaching all-time lows, those who are most vulnerable still suffer the most:

- Women experienced greater levels of sleep disruption, depression, and anxiety than men during the pandemic[34].
- Drug overdoses in the Black community have skyrocketed[35].
- Life expectancy in BIPOC communities has dropped by ~3 years[36].
- Between 2019 and 2021, proficiency in math declined by 17 percentile points for Hispanic students, 15 percentile points for Black students, and 14 percentile points for Native American students, turning the academic achievement gap into a chasm[37]. Another study by McKinsey revealed similar drops in reading proficiency[38].
- The pandemic has likely erased the last 6 years of DEI progress[39].

As I mentioned, most HR folks are generally kind, inclusive, and heart-centered, and there are multiple bright spots swinging the pendulum towards the bison. So, this isn't an indictment of HR professionals, but rather an indictment of the manner in which the eagle pervades our business logic, our corporate structures, and legacy people processes. It's an indictment of the logic that says individuals are to blame for systemic issues. It's a rebuke of victim-blaming that results from throwing apps and intranet tips at systemic problems. This is a call to end the madness.

If our nation didn't have a powerful purpose to be a place of flourishing, equity, and unity, to be a democratic and multicultural beacon for the world, then we could avoid responsibility for this systemic oppression and chalk it up to "man's inhumanity to man." But, we do. We do indeed have a noble purpose, so treating people in this way is out of integrity with who we say we are and lacks moral imagination.

It's time for the bison.

Instead of treating people like they are broken and blaming them for perishing in a toxic culture;

Instead of driving people apart through elitist and ineffective L+D approaches that presume there is nothing unique about people and ignores the liberating power of purpose and small, diverse, peer group learning;

Instead of driving people apart through anonymous reporting systems, paternalistic mentoring programs, and one-time compliance trainings;

Instead of driving people apart by allowing similarity bias to form geographic, racial, and political tribes; and

Instead of driving people who suffer mentally and physically into shame and isolation by telling them they are on their own to fix their broken selves with individual interventions;

Let's treat them like adults with souls, trauma, families, and communities; let's bring them together, empower them to heal, activate their purpose at work, and nurture our shared humanity.

Bison @Work

To do this, we must think holistically and get at the source of what people need to flourish: a balanced, *bullshit*-free work-load, living wages, flexibility, meaning, connection, and care. We all need to believe that we matter and are a part of something larger than us that matters. The bison way is one of relationships versus the eagle's outputs, of covenants versus the eagle's contracts. It is about establishing our personal covenant with our unique purpose, and with each other around a shared mission. It is the way of nurturing a healthy culture where each of us can activate and fulfill our purpose on the job, and enjoy rich connections with each other.

We must avail ourselves of the research and an emerging set of best practices, which we'll explore in greater detail in the next chapter, so that we can come together across differences to serve an aligned vision, empowering cross-functional teams to achieve common goals and objectives, and actively nurturing care, trust, and autonomy. This means multiple business and people metrics. No single business unit or function can address workload, *bullshit*, belonging, inclusion, productivity, flourishing, innovation, wellness, employee engagement, or attraction/retention. They all must align in order to create true systemic and culture change.

With this orientation, let's imagine how the bison way could look and feel by function:

Bison L+D

Work becomes a source of community, solidarity, self-discovery, fulfillment, and professional growth. People view their organization as a place where they activate their purpose, belong, continually learn, do their best work, and develop authentic relationships with diverse peers. Learning is sourced in purpose and values and happens continuously, over time, and in the flow of work versus in an external, one-time context. We center career development in each individual's purpose and values, developing purpose-shaped roles, versus lists of disconnected *bullshit* tasks.

As purposeful work is desired across the economic spectrum[40], learning is delivered in an egalitarian fashion, where people at each level in the organization and wherever they work, come together to activate their purpose and values at work. Because it is grounded in purpose, identity and relationships, and delivered over time, the concepts and skills are embodied as expressions of identity and purpose. They build upon each other, are translated into action, and are retained within their work relationships as norms and habits.

In practice, this means that peers at each level in an organization—from new hire to manager to director to vice president to senior leadership—are sorted into small groups of diverse peers. Each group then experiences a program together as a cohort, developing group agreements, learning new concepts, completing exercises that empower them to discover new aspects of their purpose and values, taking new purpose-aligned actions at work, and having an hour-long, peer-facilitated conversation together following a discussion guide.

Bison DEI

Work is compassionate, inclusive, forgiving, and is centered on belonging. People who feel like they belong are more than 3 times as likely to say they intend to stay for over 5 years[41]. Bison DEI doesn't punch white people on the nose and label them as racists. Rather, belonging and inclusion are baked into everything the company does, from people development to culture to L+D to product development to sales to finance to operations to supply chain to marketing to meeting design. As purpose, empathy, and inclusion are the foundation for diverse relationships, collaboration, hiring, development, and promotion, diverse peers learn skills together, work together, share their experiences, purposes and values, empathize with and respect each other, and form diverse, lasting, and authentic relationships.

Bison Culture

Imagine if work was fun, healing, and sourced in relationships. Imagine if people felt like they belonged, could bring their whole selves to work, genuinely liked the other people they work with, and were inspired by their impact. Imagine if diverse peers, across departments were regularly learning together and developing a sense of the organization's mission, history, structure, and interdependence of the various departments and geographies. This is possible and the results are inspiring.

When peers activate and share their purposes and values and find their unique connection to the organization's mission and values, this results in a 333% increase in alignment with the organization's mission[42], 50% more

94

meaningful work relationships[43], and a 7.4 month increase in tenure[44]. Resulting in a dynamic culture and a 3x return to shareholders[45]!

In these ways, we can recognize the transformative power of relationships and experience the healing power of community. We can nurture relationships as the foundation of leadership, learning, inclusion, culture, and health. When we cherish our relationships and lean on them, we realize that they are an ever-present well that heals us. Relationships become the foundation of our joy, growth, comfort, and laughter.

Bison Wellness

Work makes us happy and healthy. Research suggests that nurturing culture through connection, caring, and contribution is the key to our social and emotional health[46]. When diverse peers learn together, they develop high-trust relationships across differences and 94% of people feel comfortable sharing their fears and anxieties and discover new perspectives on their challenges[47]. Even more, deep connections and check-ins in their peer groups empower them to complete their stress cycles and avoid burnout[48]. Especially in light of the trauma related to the pandemic, racial justice, and white backlash, group interventions can be a meaningful driver of post-traumatic growth[49].

Further, activating purpose results in a 538% increase in emotional regulation and a 539% increase in resilience[50]. Purpose is also correlated with 32% fewer doctor's visits and 61% fewer hospital overnights[51]. When people build diverse relationships, they become socially integrated, which is a powerful driver of cognitive function[52] and longevity, resulting in an increase in the likelihood that employees reach age 85 by 41%[53]. Similarly, a meta-analysis of 148 studies on social networks and mortality revealed that people with strong social networks have a 91% greater chance of survival from disease than those with weak social networks[54].

When we combine sustained small group approaches with purpose activation, and the resulting 7+ year longevity bump that purpose provides[55], we have a powerful recipe for longevity and vitality, for "life, liberty, and the pursuit of happiness".

Guided by the Bison

With an authentic and clearly communicated vision, a culture of purpose, belonging and autonomy, work now has the potential to re-humanize us and drive national renewal. Guided by the bison, we shape business units as communities. We develop roles around souls. We build a legacy through our impact on each other, customers, communities, and the planet. The bison way begins and ends with people; people living on purpose and in deep relationship to each other are the drivers of innovation and collaboration. A culture of purpose recognizes that for any of us to thrive and belong, we must all thrive and belong.

Before the COVID-19 pandemic, this chapter may have sounded like a bunch of warm fuzzy platitudes, however, the pandemic revealed countless ways that we have been broken by the eagle. As such, the way of the bison provides nourishing food for our souls and healing for the soul of our nation. With this picture of where you and your organization might be headed if you choose to be guided by the bison, let's take a deeper dive into the twin drivers of flourishing: purpose and belonging.

Chapter 4 Summary:

- Traditional approaches to L+D, DEI, wellness, and culture are dehumanizing and ineffective, perpetuating harm and wasting billions of dollars and millions of hours a year.
- The pandemic revealed how much our children and female and BIPOC friends and colleagues are suffering, and have always suffered under the eagle.
- People strategies must be broken down and recreated from the ground up to be more social, inclusive, empathetic, and purpose-driven.
- By activating a bison-led approach to learning, DEI, wellness, and culture, we become more fulfilled and connected, reach our full potential, do our best work, and heal the soul of the nation.

Chapter 4 Reflection Questions:

- What is your experience of traditional (eagle) L+D, DEI, wellness and culture approaches?
- What possibilities do you see for your organization's impact if your people strategy was guided by the bison?
- How might you feel differently about HR if your organization was guided by the bison?
- What actions could you take to move your organization towards a more humanistic and connected people strategy?

Chapter 5

The Twin Drivers of Flourishing

Thank you for being on this journey and making it this far. I've tried to provoke and inspire you. I've tried to support these provocations with data. By this point, you may already get it. After all, it's a pretty simple message: Empower everyone to live their purpose at work and build diverse and authentic relationships. This expresses the eternal wisdom of the Golden Rule, and our ancestors, mentors, and teachers.

Although we will continue going into greater detail into the nature and mechanics of activating purpose and belonging, I invite you to hold the simplicity of this movement, and remember who you were as a child. I invite you to consider that what we are doing together here is merely remembering who we really are and that we can get back to being humans with each other.

As Robert Fulghum reminded us in his 1986 book, *All I Really Need To Know I Learned In Kindergarten,* the most important things in life were taught to us in kindergarten, like listening, sharing our gifts, respecting each others' beliefs and needs, telling the truth, asking for consent, taking responsibility for the impacts of our actions, making amends, and hugging it out. In this sense, the journey we're on as leaders, organizations, nations, a species, and planet, is a deep remembering.

The bison way is basic and it doesn't have to be hard. We need to remember who we are, realize what unique gifts we bring, and relearn how to receive the gifts of others, along with standing up for what we believe, protecting what is sacred, and repairing harm. Our wisdom traditions and wise leaders like Brené Brown, George Bernard Shaw, Thomas Friedman, Martin Luther King, Jr., and Fred Rogers all endeavor to guide us back into the simplicity of our true nature. Our essential caring, courageous, and creative nature is here, always waiting to be expressed.

"I define connection as the energy that exists between people when they feel seen, heard, valued; when they can give and receive without judgment; and when they derive sustenance and strength from the relationship."

- Brené Brown

"This is the true joy in life, being used for a purpose recognized by yourself as a mighty one, the being a force of nature, instead of a feverish, selfish little clod of ailments and grievances complaining that the world will not devote itself to making you happy. I am of the opinion that my life belongs to the whole community, and as long as I live, it is my privilege to do for it whatever I can. I want to be thoroughly used up when I die, for the harder I work, the more I live. I rejoice in life for its own sake. Life is no brief candle to me. It is a sort of splendid torch, which I've got held up for the moment, and I want to make it burn as brightly as possible before handing it on to future generations."

- George Bernard Shaw

"We used to work with our hands for many centuries; then we worked with our heads, and now we're going to have to work with our hearts, because there's one thing machines cannot, do not, never will have, and that's a heart. We're going from hands to heads to hearts."

-Thomas Friedman

"But the end is reconciliation; the end is redemption; the end is the creation of the beloved community. It is this type of spirit and this type of love that can transform opposers into friends. The type of love that I stress here is not eros, a sort of esthetic or romantic love; not philia, a sort of reciprocal love between personal friends; but it is agape which is understanding goodwill for all men."

-Martin Luther King, Jr.

"The older I get, the more convinced I am that the space between people who are trying their best to understand each other is hallowed ground."

- Fred Rogers

To activate this wisdom is to consecrate the ethics of the bison. There is an emerging set of best practices that will guide us back home to ourselves and each other, to activate tenderness, authenticity, understanding, purpose, belonging, and respect. Let's explore the research.

Research Review

The same two things that lead to a long, happy and healthy life—purpose and social integration—are also what we need to be fulfilled, creative, and productive at work. According to Edelman's 2021 Trust Barometer, employees want more purposeful work and a sense of belonging and being valued[1]. Similarly, Gartner found that workforce health depended on purpose and connection:

"What employees need is a more personal sense of purpose. When employees believe that their work is personally relevant, there is a 26% increase in the likelihood of the organization to sustain workforce health. Employees also need to feel connected to one another… Highly cohesive teams have a 37% higher likelihood of sustaining workforce health."[2]

So how do we activate purpose, belonging, and the ethics of the bison in our organizations? Two studies based on the work of my former teams at ion Learning and Imperative, illuminate the foundations of scalable culture change.

ion Learning Study Summary[3]

103 people from a large biotechnology company were placed into groups of 3-4 peers, with each group optimized for diversity. They completed a 6-module program where they learned new concepts, reflected on their purpose and values, and shared their experiences with each other in 6 hour-long small group discussions. They did this in the flow of work and over a period of time. The results of this approach are that 95% of people completed the program, 90% feel they can apply the concepts, 85% changed their behaviors, 76% embedded their understanding into daily habits, and participants reported learning 63% more because of conversations with their peers. Additionally, 98% of people experienced respect from their diverse peers, 96% experienced empathy, 96% discovered alternative perspectives to their challenges, and 94% felt comfortable discussing their anxiety and fears that distract them from work.

Imperative Study Summary[4]

This study involved 30,000+ conversations across 27 functions and 14 industries, such as professional services, finance, retail, consumer, technology, healthcare, government, education, and nonprofits. People were placed in pairs to have 5 hour-long guided video discussions to reflect on their purpose and share their work and life experiences with each other.

Before beginning the study, they found that 22% had no meaningful relationships, and that 76% of the participants' desired to develop power skills and work relationships (versus 24% who desired to develop technical skills). They found that after the intervention, participants felt 2.4 times more positive, had 2 times more friends at work, 78% felt their experience made them more successful, 71% took new actions during the program, and 52% took a new action after each conversation. Further, among participants who were unfulfilled prior to the study, 62% reported a significant increase in fulfillment in less than 3 months.

Collectively, these studies paint a picture of what we need to do to guide us back home to ourselves and each other:

A. put people in small, diverse groups of peers,
B. empower them to learn new skills and activate their purpose and values at work, and
C. share their experiences with each other in the flow of work, over time, and regardless of where they are physically located.

Let's now take a closer look at each driver of organizational flourishing: purpose and belonging.

Driver #1: Purpose

def. 'purpose': a transcendent identity beyond the concerns of self and family that includes many aspects such as one's vision for the world, mission, craft, greatest gifts, and most cherished values.

Purpose gives us access to more of ourselves and more connection to others. It serves us individually, as it is the key to our leadership, impact, fulfillment, and prosperity, AND it serves others, as it expands our identity and concern from self and family to include larger entities such as our community, company, nation, and planet. It makes us more independent and self-reliant, and also more connected and compassionate.

When we activate purpose, we come alive. We know who we are, who we belong to, who we serve, and what is ours to do. We have the clarity, confidence, and courage to do the hard, right, and unpopular things—and to do them with wisdom and compassion. We are connected to ourselves, each other, and a future of shared prosperity. We move towards each other, towards discomfort and ambiguity, and find the hidden connections and the "hallowed ground" between us. We lean on, versus lean down on, each other. We uplift each other, welcome one another's wholeness, and stand for one another's purpose and greatness—empowering each of us to feel seen, heard, valued, and experience Shaw's "true joy in life."

Further, your employees must have a connection to their own purpose in order to understand themselves as bigger than their personality, gender, skin color, and politics, and to be able to find their own unique connection to the organization's purpose. In a sense, purpose is like a muscle; it has to be developed first individually before one can begin to take on larger forms of meaning, such as an organization's mission and values. Think of the thousands of hours Stephen Curry spent practicing dribbling and shooting so that they became second nature, allowing him to focus on larger matters such as team relationships, the plays, his opponents, leadership, and a strategy to win the NBA title. Similarly, having a connection to one's own purpose is also the foundation to seeing the outside world and interacting with it as though it was a part of us, and not something outside of us.

For example, when we spend just 5 minutes connecting with our purpose, we are 4x more likely to choose to live in a diverse city[5] and also, we experience a 4x reduction in anxiety in diverse environments[6]. While this is a stark difference, it is not unexpected, as purpose is correlated with numerous prosocial attributes:

- Purpose is correlated with an increase in wisdom, transcendence, curiosity, and temperance[7].

- Purpose is correlated with an increase in gratitude, compassion, and grit[8].

- Writing about important values increases other-centeredness and reduces defensiveness[9].

- Purpose is correlated with an increase in philanthropy and volunteering by 50%[10].

- Purpose enhances reflection on past and future, increasing consideration of impact on others[11].

The reason for these dynamics is that purpose grounds us in our deepest identity, which also gives us the freedom to accept others for who they are. Perhaps it is not surprising that 3 of McKinsey's 6 aspects of an inclusive culture (authenticity, meaningful work, and camaraderie) are driven by purpose[12].

In the thousands of purpose statements generated by participants in programs I've led, such as *Man on Purpose, Purpose Challenge, Purpose Masters Program* and the *Global Purpose Expedition,* as well as in purpose activation programs I've led for LinkedIn, Monroe County Corrections, J&J, the U.S. Navy, Google, Morgan Stanley, and the U.S. Marine Corps, I have yet to encounter a purpose that isn't generative, inclusive, and good-natured. Purpose statements are usually about peace, connection, love, compassion, fun, healing, prosperity, creativity, and/or service. I've never heard anything about being # 1, or hate or division or oppression in a purpose statement.

As such, cultivating a sense of purpose is a powerful foundation for future DEI efforts. With the psychological individuation[13] and the inclusive and prosocial qualities correlated with a sense of purpose, when people encounter their microaggressions, biases, and privileges, they have less resistance transforming them. The reason for this is that when people activate their purpose, they enact a powerful shift in identity from their socialized self to their authentic self. They rely less on their ethnicity, gender, sexual orientation, nationality, income bracket, age, religion, and political party to define themselves and find a new home for their identity inside of their unique purpose and values. This is critical for every one of us to experience, especially privileged groups, so that when we develop inclusive leadership and communication practices, we see them as self-expression—as an expansion of our truest and highest sense of self and a skill set to fulfill our purpose. This is of growing importance as our teams and customers are becoming increasingly diverse.

Further, what we want for ourselves, deep down we also want for others. Especially since 97% of us value having a sense of purpose[14], when we connect with our purpose, we frequently share it with people close to us. Additionally, we recognize on some level that other folks have purposes, too. When we harness the sense of rootedness and fulfillment that purpose provides, many begin to regard purpose as a human right. Without it, we are beholden to our limiting beliefs, socialized selves, and the family trauma, systemic inequities, and internalized oppression that formed them. Accordingly, the personal liberation that comes from purpose work becomes an activist stance towards purpose itself—towards the self-actualization, prosperity, and advancement of others.

In addition to the catalytic and foundational role that purpose can play in a DEI strategy, people also want work that is personally meaningful—99% of people believe that they cannot be fulfilled in life if they are not fulfilled at work[15]. With a sense of purpose, we unlock the passion to make a generative impact on society and/or the environment, develop our gifts, and are more likely to receive a raise and promotion[16], allowing us to better provide for our families and contribute to our communities.

Until very recently, concepts like purposeful work and self-actualization were regarded as Californian and unrealistic. Millennials and Zenials, who now represent 40% of the workforce[17], have been derided as entitled babies for voicing these wants. They are not entitled babies; they are merely better at articulating our common human desire for purposeful work. Increasingly, more of us are following their lead, as 2/3 of us revisited our purpose in life during the pandemic[18].

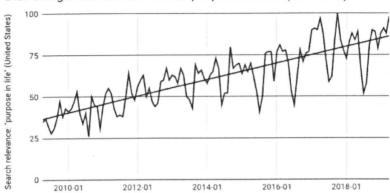

U.S. Google search relevance: "purpose in life" (4/9-4/19)

Source: Google Trends[19]

As 90% of us are willing to trade 23% of our lifetime earnings for more meaning[20], it is time to consider that purposeful work is simply what work now means to people and without purpose, work lacks a central component. Unfortunately, only 15% of people believe they can fulfill their purpose in their current roles[21]. The resulting "purpose gap"—the delta between the 90% of us who want more meaning and the 15% who think it's possible in their current roles—is a massive recruiting and retention risk for organizations.

The demand for purposeful work echoes similar shifts in consumer beliefs, as 9 of every 10 consumers say they would rather buy from a company that leads with purpose[22], and 87% of global consumers believe businesses should put at least as much emphasis on social interests as business ones[23].

The 2021 Edelman Trust Barometer confirms that we are far beyond the purpose tipping point. Employees are now the most important stakeholder in organizations (versus customers, investors, and community). 83% of all employees are now driven by purpose and values, 59% of job changers seek more fulfilling work, inclusive cultures, continuous learning, and a generative impact on society and planet, and 76% are committed to taking actions internally to produce urgent and necessary changes[24].

Further, 79% of purpose-driven employees recommend their company's products and services to others (versus 64% of people who aren't purpose-driven) and 76% recommend their company as a place to work (versus 59% of people who aren't purpose-driven). 76% of purpose-driven employees want to stay at their organization for many years (versus 63% of people who aren't purpose-driven), and 78% will do more than what's expected to help the organization succeed (versus 62% of people who aren't purpose-driven)[25].

However, purpose isn't the only thing we need to activate the ethics of bison. As we explored in the last chapter, every aspect of organizational life must move towards caring for people as connected, whole, unique, and sovereign adults, with gifts and passions that are longing to be activated and developed.

Driver #2: Belonging

"People are hard to hate up close."

—Brene Brown

We ache to belong. Whether we consider ourselves employees, kindergartners, humans, or bison, we long to belong. We have simply forgotten our nature. It's time to come back home to ourselves and our relationships. But, what does it actually mean to belong?

Belonging is the sense that you matter, that all of you is welcome, and you do not have to leave anything at the door. Alex Pentland, PhD and Oren Lederman, PhD of MIT's Human Dynamics Lab[26] have run dozens of studies on belonging, nonverbal communication, and group performance. They have discovered that belonging is not about fitting in or conforming, but about mattering and safety. It is the result of a series of behaviors or cues such as, energy, turn taking / inclusion, and intergroup communication that signal safety. Digging deeper, they found that the most effective belonging cues have these 3 qualities:

- Investment, presence, and energy that suggest the relationship is safe and the connection is important.
- Mattering, signaling that each person has dignity, worth, and their contribution is desired.
- A shared future, signaling that the relationship has a future.

Similarly, Coqual (formerly the Center for Talent Innovation) defines belonging as being composed of feeling seen, connected, supported, and proud[27]. When these elements are activated across the employee experience, then people feel safe, like they matter, can relax, and are excited to learn, grow, connect, and do their best work. As with purpose, there is a powerful belonging ROI, producing a:

- 56% increase in job performance
- 50% reduction in turnover
- 75% decrease in sick days
- 167% increase in employee net promoter score (eNPS)[28]

Now, let's explore how belonging drives organizational health in a few key people functions.

Belonging & L+D

We're not just wired to connect and belong, but to learn together. Peer learning is how most learning already happens. Research suggests that 80% of us learn as much or more from our peers than authority figures[29] and, as we have already explored, we learn 63% more from conversations in small, diverse, learning cohorts than we do from consuming information alone[30]. This is because weak ties—such as those between trainers and learners—are good for spreading information only. Habits, norms, and building a successful career require more than information transfer, but mirroring, modeling and reflection that are present in the strong ties of relationships[31]. According to McKinsey & Co., relationships empower us to find meaning and impact, as,

"...immersive, small-group sessions may not sound as sexy as a paid leave of absence to do good in the world, but they are a lot more effective at helping employees start to see the good they can do in their day-to-day work."[32]

Belonging & DEI

Belonging matters at every stage in the employee journey, and especially for new diverse hires. If diverse candidates build a wide network of diverse peers in their first 6 months, then they are more likely to receive early promotions and enjoy longer tenures[33]. Wide peer networks empower employees to develop a broader understanding of the organization and industry and bring a greater depth of knowledge and innovation to problem solving[34], thus empowering diverse hires to be more effective at work, able to build trust, and receive promotions[35]. Without belonging, organizations suffer, as they can't harvest the creativity and productivity benefits that diverse workforces foster[36].

Belonging & Wellness

As we explored in the last chapter, nurturing belonging through connection, caring, and contribution is the key to our social and emotional health[37], driving social integration that increases our life spans by 7+ years[38]. Connecting with each other also improves our mood, as every hour of social time improves your chance of having a good day[39]. Further, regular check-ins empower us to complete our stress cycles and avoid burnout[40].

So, how do we structure experiences to activate purpose and belonging? We put people in small, diverse groups where they learn about themselves and each other, develop new skills, and take actions over time. Now, we'll explore an emerging set of best practices to do that.

The Science of Social Learning

Small group interventions are the future of learning and behavior change. Groups enable behavior change through social support[41], the formation of group norms[42], group identity[43], social identities[44], and through group feedback and being challenged[45]. As Nick Craig and Scott Snook observed in the Harvard Business Review, "You can't get a clear picture of yourself without trusted friends acting as mirrors."[46]

When small groups are designed in such a manner that we feel safe and can share uncomfortable feelings, we experience fewer feelings of isolation, alienation, blame, and stigma due to past mistakes[47]. As people are engaged in supporting each other, sharing vulnerably, and skillfully challenging each other over time, their beliefs, behaviors, and underlying intuitions expand their sense of group identity and moral reasoning[48].

Further, in virtual and global organizations with team members in various locations, those who nurture authentic connections between members and empower them to collaborate around a shared task, increase team performance[49].

Given the power that groups have to shift behavior (for better or worse), we must bring a great deal of care and attention to how we form these groups. The size, composition, and duration of groups, as well as how people learn together, are critical elements of creating a successful social learning experience.

Group Size

For every person added to a group, there is a loss of depth and a gain in perspective[50]. Additionally, larger groups (> 6 people) face logistical difficulties in selecting a time to meet, and there is a loss of conversational depth, as people have less time to share their experiences. Conversely, a group of 2 people is less likely to bring a breadth of perspectives needed for a rich exchange. Also, the connection, understanding, and norms that form between 2 people aren't reinforced by a third or fourth person, so the dyad runs the risk of their connection, learning, and transformation being merely a private matter—something unique to them and outside of the broader culture—versus part of the broader culture. To conclude, it is likely that the optimal "Goldilocks condition" for a peer learning group's size is 3-6 people.

Group Composition

To create a climate of safety and full expression in the group, it is important that there are as few power dynamics as possible[51]. This means that each group must be composed of peers at roughly the same level and without direct reporting relationships. Given the limited size of a group (3-6), when a person is placed in a group, it is important that the perspective they bring is diverse and unique. Research suggests that optimizing groups for diversity, especially in relation to gender[52] and ethnicity[53], yields better learning and behavioral outcomes.

Gordon Allport's 1954 "contact hypothesis" and several decades of subsequent research confirms that the more contact people have with those who are different, the greater they understand them and feel connected to them[54]. A meta-analysis of over 500 studies on intergroup contact revealed that interacting with people who have different backgrounds reduces out-group prejudice 94% of the time[55].

Of particular interest to organizations is that fostering divides across function and geography is also critical, as it breaks down silos, enhances institutional knowledge transfer, and empowers diverse candidates to build a wide professional network[56]. This has become especially important during the pandemic, as according to a recent Microsoft study, "firm-wide remote work caused the collaboration network of workers to become more static and siloed, with fewer bridges between disparate parts."[57]

Program Duration, Size, and Scope

Because people forget 90% of what they learn within 7 days after a one-time training[58], it is critical that learning is spaced out over time, so that it can be reinforced, woven into identity, experienced in the flow of work, and empowers diverse relationships to form. Research suggests that the optimal number of sessions for a social learning experience is 5-6 sessions[59,60]. Further, as we've explored, in order to effect culture change across an entire population such as an organization, at least 25% of the population must adopt a new belief or practice a new behavior before a broader culture shift begins[61].

While the aforementioned research is relatively new, building diverse relationships around a shared purpose has been central to many of our greatest innovations and proudest moments as a nation.

From Farm Aid in the 1980's, to the Jigsaw method to racially integrate Texas schools in the 1970's, and to the diverse collaboration that put Neil Armstrong on the moon in the 1960's, we continually come back to the same conclusion: we are better, kinder, and stronger together. Given the power of purpose and small, diverse, peer-learning groups, are you ready to unleash the potential of your people and transform your organization?

In the next chapter, we'll explore how to move these best practices into action.

Chapter 5 Summary:

- There is an overwhelming amount of research that suggests activating purpose and belonging drive flourishing for employees, customers, and investors.
- Like purpose, belonging must also be cultivated across L+D, DEI, and wellness functions.
- The current best practice to unlock individual and organizational flourishing is to bring peers together in small, diverse learning groups to activate their purpose at work and share their experiences with each other.
- Organizations and nations thrive when diverse people work together towards a common purpose.

Chapter 5 Reflection Questions:

- When have you felt like you truly belonged?
- What does it feel like in your body to truly belong? What emotions do you experience when you belong?
- Describe a time when you were working on a team with a sense of shared purpose and mutual respect? What emotions arise as you recall this time?
- How would activating your purpose on the job and having multiple diverse and fulfilling relationships at the end of your first year in a new organization impact you?

Chapter 6

Elements and Emergence

"*You're playing—right?*" said Miles, the captain of the Columbia Business School Rugby Team.

"Huh? Na man, I'm just here to watch. Geno invited me," I responded.

"Well, mate," he said in his British accent, "We need you, we're short men. Have you played before?"

"Nope. I've literally never even seen a game. I'm just here to watch. I would be of no use to you."

"We need you. We're short men."

After a long pause, I said, "Ok. What do I need to know? Do you have extra gear? I'm gonna need some Gatorade."

"I'll find you gear. Grab Gatorade across the street. Geno will explain the rest in the cab."

"We need you," is a powerful phrase. It awakened something in me. It feels good to be needed. It feels even better to say "yes" to meet that need.

In that cab ride from campus to the pitch on Roosevelt Island, Geno explained the game as best he could. Unfortunately, I was hungover, out of shape, and started cramping up during warm ups. However, by the time the opening whistle blew, a switch turned on. I crashed the first ruck (a fight over the ball on the ground), popped up, crashed the next one, and so on. In those first 10 minutes, I was in about every play, in a flow state, where my sense of self and identity fell away and there was only the game. It brought me back to playing schoolyard tackle football. Just the endless joy of play. Present moment awareness, bodies crashing, full exertion—pure and simple fun.

I caught the rugby bug, and the rest is history. I joined the team, got in shape, earned a starting position, took a leadership role, and fell in love with the sport and the culture. I loved my teammates, the practices, the matches, the collaboration, the road trips, tournaments, the songs, and awards. I loved the sense of unity, of coming together with teammates from all corners—from Africa, Asia, Latin America, the Middle East, and Europe—around our shared purpose: victory and camaraderie. This made the intense training and injuries of the sport feel important, even sacred. I was always a little sad when I pulled out my stitches, as they held fond memories of the match and my mates.

In my second year of business school, my friend Gaby and I started and coached the women's rugby club to share our love of the sport and culture with all of our classmates. It won't surprise you to hear that most of my best friends were once rugby teammates. I share this experience because it approximated the purpose of our diverse nation—bringing diverse people together around a common purpose—as well as the challenge now facing all leaders: to act boldly despite having imperfect information and no precedent.

When I said "yes" and got in that cab, the die was cast, even though I had only a rough outline of what I was saying "yes" to. I learned the elements of the sport, of course, but the series of events, the joy, the creativity, the connections, the sense of belonging and mattering, and all the new ways I was able to grow, lead, receive, contribute after saying "yes", no one could have predicted.

You are being asked to say "yes" to bringing forth all you have within you to lead and co-create the future.

The old way of leading and developing people no longer works. Our understanding of the economy is far different than what is taught in traditional business education and corporate trainings. The "American Dream" no longer fits the data and doesn't feed our souls. Customer, employee, and investor demands have changed dramatically. The democratic institutions upon which our economy depends, and that we considered immutable, are crumbling faster by the minute. The planet is becoming more hostile to life. If there ever was a time to boldly venture into the unknown with imperfect information, it is now.

Unfortunately, activating an organizational, cultural, and leadership transformation is not going to follow a staid linear progression. Our cosmos is dynamic, relational, omni-centric, emergent, and co-creative. Eagle leadership is anything but; it's linear in its thinking, contractual in practice, and exploitative in impact. Whereas bison leadership is responsive; it meets the dynamism, interconnection, and emergence as it is, and with common cause and agility.

Moreover, every organization in every industry and size/maturity is different, so there is no "one-size fits all" approach to culture change. Like everything else that matters in your life—your marriage, family, and community—saying "yes" to this adventure means paying attention to what is needed now and responding with both care and courage. When you say "yes," the future you step into will demand much more of you than you are currently capable of fulfilling, and it will be far more rewarding than your current self is capable of envisioning.

The reason for this is that, by definition, the shape of a purpose-driven organization is unknowable until the purpose of each person in your organization comes alive and arises anew, moment by moment. This is a profound paradigm shift from the eagle's top-down expertise and knowledge approach to the bison's bottom-up purpose and agility approach. As Carlos Rey PhD, Jon San Cristobal Velasco PhD and Juan Almandoz PhD assert in *Purpose-driven Organizations* (2019)[1],

"...the fulfillment of personal purpose within the organizational purpose is the essence of a truly purpose-driven organization... Strategy is based no longer on accurate predictions of the future, but on developing dynamic skills and capabilities that allow individuals and organizations to adapt rapidly. In this changing and uncertain world, employees no longer find solace in top-down definitions of organizational purpose... The new logic of purpose requires people to lead the evolutionary process of their own purpose at work."

As you are transformed by your purpose, your people are also transformed and turning on. You're flipping switches in unique human hearts. You're weaving the social fabric of your company. You are activating oblique and emergent logic, whereby the organization's purpose and each individual's purpose interact and innovate to meet and co-create the future. As the founder of Bimbo Bakeries aptly observed, "...the company has a soul made up of the souls of each of its workers."[2] You are unique as is everyone else who will discover and activate their purpose in your organization. Once activated, they will bring their fullness to work—their emotions, creativity, ethics, pain, dreams and wounds—and in so doing, they will change you, your organization, and your future for the better.

Your people will be empowered to voice their dissenting opinions, wild ideas, and speak truth to power, so you are in effect licensing your employees to cause "good trouble" as John Lewis might say. This means that, on occasion, you will be called to look at your lack of integrity. Because your employees will be empowered by having activated their purpose and values in their small, diverse groups, and because you've shown them your vulnerability and heartbreak, inviting them to bring their whole selves to work, they will reveal weaknesses in your strategy, ethics, and leadership. Because they are enlivened and empowered, they will tell when your plans aren't credible and when you are not being authentic. You're saying "yes" to authenticity and courage, to becoming fully alive, on purpose, warts and all. You're saying "yes" to the emergent possibilities of human creativity, and the burning away of everything in your life and organization that is unaligned with our bison nature.

You're going to make mistakes and maybe even cause or reveal a scandal. You'll learn from them, clean them up, and try it again with new knowledge. As beautiful as our Constitution is, it was not complete when it was written. It needed amendments. Plenty of them. So will you. You will never be done with activating the purpose of your people and organization. When you die or retire, there will be a long list of things that you wish you got to do. It's important to accept the imperfection and implicit incompleteness of this journey, so that you can just be here right now and create the conditions for everyone to play the game.

Check in: As you approach the end of this book and start moving towards action, you might be feeling a good deal of fear. We've covered a lot of ground. Let's be frank, we're proposing an entirely new economic, cultural, and organizational paradigm—a shift from command, control, and exploit to empower, connect, and create.

Shepherding such a transition is a sticky wicket, to say the least, especially given the aforementioned political, economic, social, and ecological dysfunction, economic pressure, the unique personalities in your organization, their varying levels of growth and openness, and the simple fact that your job provides you and your family with food, housing, and healthcare. Taking a stand for a better world takes courage and resilience. To that end, please reach out to your book club and/or your peers in the Purpose Work Nation community to share what you are experiencing, or contact my team at Unity Lab to develop your plan for building buy-in. As a reminder, if you notice your mental health declining, seek immediate help from a mental health practitioner.

However, there are many joys inherent in this approach. You will be nourished by the changes along the way, the thrill of the game, the big wins and small gains. When roles fill quickly from employee referrals, and people turn down bigger compensation packages to join your organization, your spine will tingle, you'll grin and give thanks. When journalists start asking you about how you did it, you'll giggle and say, "Me? Yeah, right... Us and some luck."

So, what is your next step? Although this book is not a how-to manual, it's still important to have a rough outline of the important elements of the new reality we're moving into, so we can take good guesses about what to do, how to do it, and when. Consider the following paragraphs a cab ride to that first rugby pitch. Your actual plan of action will depend on your unique organization, the needs of the people you serve, and those you call in to help guide the process. As you dump everything on the table in this *Apollo 13* moment and consider what's the right approach for your organization, I want to share a handful of key elements that may be useful as you guide your organization into the era of the bison.

Element #1: Purpose to the People

Purpose is a human right. It is our key to a life of fulfillment, vitality, connection, innovation, and prosperity. Everyone has a right to discover and activate it. And when they do, everybody wins. Employees are happier, healthier, and more creative, connected, productive, and committed. Investors receive better returns. Accordingly, employee purpose is the foundation of authentic individual and organizational transformation, and you have the power to enable it at scale. Although we're empowering everyone to activate their purpose, it is important that the invitation is made from a place grounded, not just in the idea of purpose, but from purpose. As such, consider beginning purpose activation work first with your executive leadership team (ELT), empower them to share openly about their experience, and then engage the rest of the company. Finally, weave purpose and values' reflection into onboarding and every DEI, L&D, wellness, and culture initiative.

What if, along the way, you discover that someone's purpose cannot be fulfilled in any way at your company? This happens. In my experience, it occurs about 5% of the time, and yet the net effect of activating purpose is an average increase in tenure of 7.4 months[3]. So, not to worry.

You are going to lose a few folks, but these good people will be thankful for their experience when their purpose is fulfilled in their next chapter. Of course, when compared to the alternative—denying them the right to activate their purpose and allowing the *bullshit*, toxicity, and inequity to remain, wasting human potential and the opportunity to be part of national renewal—it is a small price to pay. As such, better questions to ask are: What if we don't empower them to activate their purpose and they stick around? What kind of representatives of our brand would they be? How would they lead? How would they impact tenure, DEI goals, and morale?

Element #2 Golden Gate Bridge

As we've explored, people learn best together in small, diverse, peer-learning groups, over time, and in the flow of work. They also need "big tent" events to invite them on the journey, to celebrate their achievements, and to establish a collective sense that something new just happened among everyone. Picture the Golden Gate Bridge with its two tall towers supporting the entire bridge. Think of San Francisco as the current state of your business and Marin County as the future. Think of the bridge as a chronological line from shore to shore, with a pre-program leadership, team, and culture assessment and a group matching survey (to optimize the peer-learning groups for diversity) completed before the first tower.

The first tower is a "big tent" event that introduces the program objectives and guides / facilitators, and is an opportunity for participants to understand the logistics, meet in their small groups, and get their questions answered. Think of the 5 small group sessions being stretched between the two towers.

The second tower / "big tent" event is designed to recap the program, celebrate the wins, distribute certificates, and enroll folks in their next learning journey. The post-program assessment is then completed after the second tower / "big tent" event, which enables you to measure their progress in beliefs and behaviors versus the pre-program assessment.

Consider that this approach, especially when centered in purpose and values reflection is a blunt instrument that immediately goes to work on transforming your entire organization. People become more connected to themselves, their peers, and your organization. Social and emotional health improves. People are learning new skills and practicing inclusion in their small groups on a consistent basis.

Element #3 Inclusive and Digitally Native Culture

Most organizations are located in urban and suburban areas where housing is frequently expensive, making convening in the office a physical and economic barrier that often means long commutes and a negative impact on the well-being of your employees and families.

In an ideal world, there would be abundant affordable housing within biking distance so folks could convene safely and easily. Until that is the case, your approach must be digitally native, such that wherever folks are, they can participate and contribute on a level playing field, (e.g., a Zoom room versus a live training on-site). This also breaks down silos between functions and teams spread across multiple locations, widens the pool for attracting diverse talent, and makes the organization more agile and adaptive to future scenarios (e.g., pandemics, climate change, shifts in public policy, etc.).

In addition to social learning approaches in small, diverse groups, also consider virtual events that have no immediately applicable economic end and are designed purely for fun. People need to laugh and connect. Consider delivering events that enable storytelling, show and tell, making art together, improv, 1:1 interviews in breakouts, games, and mad libs. These sorts of digitally native culture activities ensure equitable participation and contribute towards creation of the company's culture.

Element #4 Company as a Community with a Mission

You might have begun to notice that the bison way is redefining what work is and what it means to us. A job is no longer a contract to perform a faceless task at a soulless company. Rather it is both a covenantal mission and a mutually-satisfying, sustainable contract of employment to fulfill one's purpose at work. It is about joining a community in service of a greater mission AND entering into a contract for a living wage and benefits that improves the financial, physical, psychological, and social health of all parties. However, a community cannot form without a mission—the company's promise to deliver its desired impact, live its values, and be guided by its origin story—so these also need to be developed, embodied, and communicated. Only then can a community be considered to be properly consecrated.

It is also important to renew the mission periodically. Use each all-hands and business unit gathering as an opportunity to renew your mission. For example, exalt the impact of the work on customers, society, and planet, highlighting the commitment, community, and contribution that made it possible. Distribute the facilitation of these events among diverse people at all levels, so folks feel they are all represented and are co-creating and achieving the mission.

Instead of announcing promotions via email, induct the person via a more public ceremony, by exalting how they exhibit the company's values and highlighting their own purpose and passions. Invite others to share how this person has impacted them personally or made a difference for customers or the community. To engender a sense of collaboration and shared success in this new role, encourage the recently promoted person to vulnerably share their purpose, areas for growth, and the help they will need to be successful in their new role.

Occasionally, you'll find yourself on the proverbial ropes (e.g., a business downturn, loss of key talent, scandal, or some external political, economic and/or environmental malady beyond your control). Use this as an opportunity to renew and be guided by your mission and values. Turn to the mission and values and ask for guidance on how to shepherd the company/community through the dark forest. For example, instead of announcing layoffs—sending the message that certain people are expendable—communicate confidence that "we're going to make it through this together" and so the company is temporarily cutting all salaries by 90% over the living wage baseline (~$70k/yr in 2022). It's critical that senior management shares equally (if not more than others) in the temporary sacrifice. During the early days of the COVID-19 pandemic, the companies that did this engendered greater loyalty[4].

Element #5 Purposeful Leadership

Under this new paradigm of collective flourishing, everyone in leadership becomes a steward of the company's mission and values. Their job responsibilities now include contextualizing work in terms of its impact and the company's mission, values, and origin story, attending to the purpose and career development of everyone on their team, and empowering authentic connection among them.

This means leaders model and share their purpose and find their own unique expression of the company's values. This means contextualizing priorities, initiatives, and individual contributions in terms of the mission and the impact on customers, society, and planet. This means we activate everyone's purpose at work, and co-create a purpose-led professional development plan with each team member. It means holding folks accountable to their purpose and career path. It means we tell stories and encourage others to tell stories about our challenges and successes. It means exalting the accomplishments of teams, and on occasion, nurturing good-natured competition between teams, all in service of the shared mission.

This means that leaders take on (instead of delegating) the role of hosting, where we ensure everyone gets what they need to flourish. We attend to the betweenness of things, nurturing connections between people, developing relationships across in-groups and out-groups, and empowering and sponsoring diverse candidates. This is the work that creates wide bridges throughout the company, dissolving bottlenecks, building trust, improving information transfer, breaking down silos, and empowering innovation.

This also means expanding the ELT to include a Chief Purpose Officer (CPO), someone responsible for the ongoing realization of individual and organization purpose. Do not pile the new culture and purpose priorities onto someone who already has an existing role and responsibilities. Hire at least one new person whose only goal is to support purpose and impact, ensuring that all culture change work is social, substantial, and sustained, impacting at minimum 25% of each business unit, seniority level, and function[5], and is developed over the course of many years. It means aligning senior management with the goals of the Chief Purpose Officer by tying roughly half of the ELT's performance and compensation goals to the health of the community (e.g., engagement, fulfillment, tenure, CSR, social and emotional health, and DEI hiring and promotion goals).

It means administering the table stakes: CSR reports, transparent compensation and promotion policies, paying living wages (>4x rent/mortgage, <30 minute commute), empowering flex schedules, mental health services, 3+ months of required paid parental leave for all parents. Once the table stakes are in place, the organization can be considered reasonably purpose-aligned. To stay purpose-accountable consider becoming a B Corp and conducting and publishing an annual B Corp audit.

Of course, the process of developing people and culture is never done, and it is never purely an internal affair. Much like bison, organizations also exist in relationship to, and are part of, their surroundings. As such, it is incumbent for organizations to address the broader culture, environment, and society by leveraging its voice, brand and buying power, as companies such as Salesforce, Delta Airlines, and Patagonia do quite regularly, to shift the nation towards reckoning, repair, reconciliation, redemption, and renewal. This takes the form of quickly and wisely speaking out when the company's values are being desecrated with respect to emerging issues related to racial justice, climate change, universal healthcare, voting / electoral integrity, infrastructure, parental leave, etc. Further, it is critical to support organizations such as Business for America (bfa.us) and IssueOne (issueone.org) that protect our democracy and civic virtues, and affirm a mutualistic and high integrity connection between our economic and our democratic institutions.

Element #6 Triage from the Heart

There will be hard moments. Of course, there always have been and these last few years have been extremely difficult, to say the least. Perhaps you have noticed you're developing a skill set in crisis management. That's great. Accordingly, it's good to have a framework for moving through future crises, which are guaranteed, e.g., climate change.

In every culture there are acute issues, such as missed DEI targets, low retention, burnout, pay inequity, low engagement, parents not returning from parental leave, AND systemic / cultural issues, such as income inequality, systemic racism, sexism, workism, hyperindividualism, homophobia, political polarization, erosion of trust, lack of transparency, and poorly developed power skills (e.g., critical thinking, emotional intelligence, conflict resolution, purposeful leadership, etc.). Systemic issues cause acute issues. And, sometimes they collide and overlap in a perfect storm resulting in collective trauma and/or scandal.

Collective trauma is the emotional, psychological, and cultural response to the immediate loss of something we hold sacred (e.g., 9/11, George Floyd's murder, the January 6th attack on the Capitol, a disgruntled employee shooting up an office). Scandal is when acute and/or systemic issues are revealed publicly, such as a sexual harassment suit, corruption, BIPOC employees filing a discrimination suit, harmed customers filing suit, etc.

Each acute and systemic issue needs to be addressed uniquely and simultaneously, versus sequentially.

- Acute culture issues need expert outside facilitators and consultants to immediately release the pressure, give people the place to speak, share their experiences, heal, grieve, learn new skills, and practice them together. Each manager also needs an immediate intervention in order to effectively and compassionately hold space for each of their team member's experience and empower them with individual resources (e.g., paid time off, therapy, etc.), and social resources (e.g., support groups, ERGs, etc.) to process the acute issue.
- Systemic issues need to be dealt with in a swift, substantial, and sustained fashion by committing resources, and leveraging scalable and effective culture change methods to deepen relationships and develop new beliefs, behaviors, and skills.
- Collective trauma and scandal require the aforementioned responses to the acute and systemic issues, as well as an immediate public acceptance of responsibility, disclosure of the amends being made, a plan to address the acute and systemic issues, the amount of financial resources being committed, the cadence of reporting on the commitment, and hiring an outside firm to hold them accountable to it.

So, where to begin? How can you implement and leverage these elements? That depends on your company size, industry, maturity, etc., but these matter far less than the approach you take to begin the conversation. That said, if you're currently embroiled in a scandal, then start with the triage process described above. If you aren't in the middle of a scandal and are intent on activating bison ethics in your organization, I invite you to be transparent and humble in your approach, trusting that the hearts, minds, and souls of your people will rise to meet each challenge ahead. Your approach could follow this progression of stages:

Stage #1: Humbly Make This Invitation

Share your vision for becoming a new kind of company, one driven by an inspiring purpose, where social, economic, and environmental impact is generative and quantifiable, where power and wealth are more equitably distributed, where culture is deliberately crafted, where work is fun, where everyone fulfills their potential, where learning is social and ongoing, AND also admit that you are unsure exactly what this all looks like.

Share that:

- It begins with activating our individual purposes and values together, building deeper relationships, and then collectively asking who we are for the world.
- It's going to be a long journey with no known destination, so we welcome all wild ideas and dissenting opinions.
- It will be messy, we'll make mistakes, and may even reveal a scandal or two, but together we'll learn from them, do better tomorrow, and celebrate the transformation.
- If you're in for the adventure, join us. We're going to begin a process as a whole company to activate our individual purposes and bring them to work.
- If this doesn't sound fun or purposeful, then we understand. We will be sad to lose you, but we'll help you find your next job and ensure a smooth transition.

Stage #2: Administer

Then hire your CPO and activate employee purpose in small, diverse groups, beginning with the ELT, then the front-line managers, then everyone else. Equip your CPO with the power and resources to deliver the wellness, DEI, and CSR table stakes, and align incentives for senior leaders with the goals of the CPO. Next, weave purpose and values activation into existing onboarding, leadership development, DEI, wellness, and culture efforts.

Stage #3: Co-create and Consecrate the Organization's Mission & Values

After the ELT has developed a connection to their individual purpose and values, hire a facilitator (see Appendix A) to convene the ELT to either refresh the company's mission, values, and origin story or generate a first draft. Your facilitator will move you through a process with questions such as:

- What is our origin story?
- What are the values we can discern from this story?
- What values do we most see in action?
- What behaviors will we not tolerate under any circumstances?
- If we were about to be acquired by a private equity firm, would we fight to stay independent? If so, why? If not, what would we need to change our minds?
- Is the net impact of our operations generative, after all social, economic and environmental externalities are accounted for?
- As it currently functions, should our company continue to exist?
- Which of the UN's Sustainable Development Goals are we best suited to impact?
- What must we change to truly be the best solution to advance these goals?

- If we were guided by a higher purpose and a generative strategy worthy of the resources consumed, what are the very first things we should do?

Then share the ELT's aggregated answers to these questions with the whole company and invite anonymous employee feedback. Review the ELT's answers and employee feedback and formulate a revised draft of the mission and values that will guide the company over the next 2-3 years, after which it will again be revisited or reimagined.

With a "good enough" mission and values in place, consecrate the mission and values. This means dedicating the company to the mission and values in feel, form, function, and shape. How you consecrate them depends on your answers to these questions:

- How do our values guide our interactions? Meeting design? Team structures?
- How must our business model evolve to express our mission?
- How do our values guide our approach to client service?
- How does the mission impact the local community? Our country? The planet?
- How do our values shape our all-hands gatherings, events and culture?
- How do our values tangibly express themselves in the design of our offices and locations? What do we hear? See? Feel? Sense?
- What does it mean to be an employee, a member of a community, devoted to a mission?
- What is a values-led approach to the entire employee experience / lifecycle?

Stage #4: Empower Teams to Align Key Business Processes with the Mission and Values and Remove *Bullshit*

Once employee purpose activation is complete, ask the leaders of each business line and function to come up with a business and culture vision for how they could be reimagined with the mission, values, and market trends in mind. To build community buy-in and shared success, review these business unit and functional visions at a series of all-hands meetings with a public commitment to helping each employee develop a career path that fulfills their purpose.

It's critical that people feel their employment is secure, especially since roughly 50% of current roles and responsibilities are *bullshit*[6], meaning having no real purpose or positive impact, could disappear without anyone noticing, and often include functions such as subordinating others, box ticking, and duct-taping broken processes. It's critical to begin a process of unpacking and hauling out the *bullshit*. Invite employees to share the processes and interactions that energetically drain them, and voice their dissenting opinions and the synergies they see. Invite them to question job roles and responsibilities that are unaligned with the organization's mission and values, or are otherwise *bullshit*. Share out the aggregated feedback and empower each business line and functional leader to incorporate the feedback and revise their team vision and roles.

Business unit and functional leaders then develop a 2-3 year plan to implement the revised mission and values, with quarterly updates that measure progress and integrate team and customer feedback and emerging market realities. Align the team's performance and compensation with the plan, AND ensure that culture development metrics are given equal weight to business strategy. When in doubt, trust people and empower them to take risks. Have faith that people's purpose and values will rise to meet the challenges and uncertainties.

The Garden of Emergence

However, what you actually do next (versus the progression above) depends on your listening, tending, and intuiting. As a leader, it's helpful to think of yourself as a gardener of a diverse ecology. As gardeners till the soil and pay attention to sunlight, water, growth, fruiting, and flowering, as well as to weeds, disease, and overgrowth, leaders tend a space where every person can discover and activate their purpose on the job, and remove the *bullshit* in the way of their flourishing.

"A gardener grows nothing, plants do that—that's what plants are designed to do, and they're really good at it. But the gardener's role is not unimportant...all the things the gardener does to create an environment and ecosystem allows the plants to do what they do, and do it very, very well."

- **Ret. Four Star General Stanley McChrystal**[7]

In addition to planting, pruning, watering, and staking off the perimeter, we must pay attention to how each plant is responding to changes in the other plants and the environment. Do they need more or less sun? More or less water? Are they avoidant of dissimilar plants? Or do they flourish best together like the three sisters (corn, squash, and beans)?

Most importantly, as every master gardener knows, you're not raising plants, so much as you are cultivating soil. Soil... Soul... Humus... Human... Cultivate... Culture... Habitat... Habits...

You are paying attention to the soulfulness present in professional relationships. Are your people vulnerable? Caring? Innovative? Do they get excited? Are they sharing their wild ideas and dissenting opinions? Are they sharing about their families and struggles? Are they growing? What is the feeling, the sentiment, the unseen and unspoken, the betweenness in the life and work of your people? Are they bringing their whole selves to work? Are they enthusiastically contributing to the culture? Do they claim the company's mission as their own and innovate on its behalf? Is there a palpable sense of aliveness?

For example, if diverse folks still aren't being promoted or people still aren't returning from parental leave—guess what? You could have sexist, racist, ageist, ableist, and heteronormative biases poisoning the soil. If you grow healthy soil, and pay attention to the needs of each plant, they will flourish.

Cultivate belonging and purpose. Consecrate the mission and values. Celebrate soul, empathy, creativity, courage, and vulnerability. Give each person what they need to thrive. Compassionately weed out *bullshit*.

When you do, you will have created a place where everyone belongs, is cared for, and feels fulfilled. Imagine what kind of partner and parent a team member will be after a workday full of belonging, learning, creativity, and fulfillment. Imagine how they will communicate with their loved ones while preparing for work in the morning. Imagine how they will show up with their extended family and in their community.

Imagine yourself responsible for having begun this process, for listening to your people, empowering them to activate their purpose, and making your organization a place where everyone can flourish and collectively prosper. Imagine facing uncomfortable truths about yourself and your leadership. Imagine learning from these lessons, growing and transforming into a more full version of yourself, alive and on purpose as a leader.

Imagine a country where this is the new normal—where hundreds of thousands of leaders like you have activated purpose and belonging at scale. Imagine that we are successful—and purpose and belonging are now givens.

What's possible now? How might our culture shift? How might this impact our democratic and civic virtues? Healthcare? Education? Transportation? Community development? Public safety?

Whatever your vision is for this new world, it begins with you and your organization. We cannot wait. As we've explored, the most vulnerable people in your care are suffering under your watch. The republic is falling. And, it is not possible to have it all figured out in advance. We must move. Now. We Need You.

Chapter 6 Summary:

- These are unprecedented times requiring bold action, humility, trust, purpose, agility, constant learning, and collaboration versus expertise, knowledge, and hierarchy.
- Begin your organization's transformation with these elements: employee purpose activation, a Golden Gate Bridge pedagogy, an inclusive and digitally native culture strategy, redefining a company as a community with a mission, purposeful leadership practices, and triaging crises from the heart.
- The path to change varies for each organization, but may follow a progression through stages, such as: 1. Humbly making the invitation, 2. Administering employee purpose activation, hiring a CPO and enacting the table stakes, 3. Consecrating the organization's mission and values, 4. Aligning the business with the mission and values and weeding out *bullshit*.
- Good leaders are gardeners.

Chapter 6 Reflection Questions:

- When have you ventured boldly with imperfect information?
- As you think about shifting from a top-down strategy and expertise orientation to a purpose and agility orientation, what fears and concerns arise?
- What fears and concerns arise about leading with vulnerability and humility (e.g., sharing with your board and team that you don't have total clarity and you'll have to discover it together)?
- If you were to allow the metaphor of the gardener to guide your leadership, what new actions would you take at work? What *bullshit* roles and responsibilities would you need to transform or remove?

Conclusion

Without the bison's guidance, the eagle will continue to desecrate all we hold dear. It entrenches political gridlock, hatred, inequality, and violence, and makes it impossible to respond to our escalating crises (democratic, biological, psychological, ecological, economic, and cultural). Without the bison, the eagle will continue to segregate our communities, siphon wealth into the coffers of the already wealthy, defund our healthcare, education, and infrastructure, and imperil our ability to co-lead the world's interdependent economy and ecology.

Guided by the bison, we recognize we are stewards of our company's soul and our nation's renewal.

Guided by the bison, we acknowledge that diversity is our strength, purpose is a human right, and a journey of reckoning, repair, and redemption is our nation's spiritual path. The workplace is where we congregate to serve and empower others, to activate our unique purpose, fulfill our potential, nurture community, and achieve our mission. We bring the spirit of the bison home with us and let it guide our family and civic life. In so doing, we activate the purpose of this nation, repair the damage from our past, and achieve redemption.

To claim our role as leaders in healing the soul of the nation, we have to

- SOBERLY meet our past and present as it is,
- adopt the bison as a SYMBOL of our leadership and nation,
- understand the STAKES of this perilous moment,
- re-humanize our organizations with an ethos of communal and holistic CARE,
- make thorough use of the two most powerful TOOLS at our disposal (purpose activation and small, diverse group learning), and
- deploy the key elements of transformation, while listening and attending to our people's needs and the emerging market with AGILITY.

A brief summary:

SOBRIETY. In Chapter 1, we explored business as a religion, villain, and savior, and learned that all the harms of white supremacy are maintained by our collective efforts. Leaders must soberly meet this reality as it is, and also acknowledge the enormous power of business, and then take responsibility to steward our culture toward the collective good and national renewal.

SYMBOL. In Chapter 2, we confronted the sad truth that our nation's soul is gasping for breath. The hyperindividualism of the eagle is dehumanizing, dividing, dominating, and dispossessing us faster by the day. A new symbol must now guide us as leaders and as a nation into the next chapter of our shared story: the bison.

STAKES. In Chapter 3, we faced the cultural consequences of the eagle: the continued dissolution of our democratic institutions, decline of our social and emotional health, fraying of the social fabric and public trust, and the increasing likelihood of racially and politically motivated violence.

CARE. In Chapter 4, we explored a rehumanized vision of key people functions, weaving the ethics of the bison into every aspect of the employee experience and each people function–L&D, DEI, wellness, talent, culture.

TOOLS. In Chapter 5, we examined purpose and belonging as the foundation of individual and organization health, and learned that purpose activation in small, diverse learning groups is an effective and scalable methodology for change.

AGILITY. In Chapter 6, we explored six elements to evolve our organization, consecrate our purpose, and meet the needs of our people and the emerging world. We learned we cannot afford to analyze, debate, and wait; we're not able to figure it all out in advance. We must move—Now.

National renewal depends on the leadership of business. We have the tools, elements, and a good enough plan to take the next step: **Activate employee purpose and belonging.** *Most importantly, do it now—do not wait.* Trust that the hearts and minds of your people will rise to the challenge.

"How wonderful it is that nobody need wait a single moment

before starting to improve the world."

- Anne Frank

Everything we hold sacred depends upon it. The nation needs you. Your children and grandchildren are asking. The world is watching.

Epilogue

"This is our nation," I said to myself as tears flooded my eyes.

It was a warm summer evening, the kind I fondly remember from my youth in the Midwest—a moment of liminal expanse, of *kairos*, of being beyond normal time and part of eternity—a place in-between places, a place between playing tag and lightning bugs, between hot dogs and ice cream. Was there scotch and ice in my tumbler that night? Yes. Did I eat a couple mushrooms before I left the house? You betcha. The veil, as they say, was thin.

My eyes softened and the sinews of my environs came to view: with diversity, goodwill, connection, and creative self-expression. I felt a sense of oneness and jubilance. I was witness to a nation's promise—from many, one—all of us created equal—life, liberty, and the pursuit of happiness. Was this the "beloved community" Dr. King foresaw? Was this what Maslow experienced among the Blackfoot people?

Fireworks don't do it for me. The Pledge of Allegiance doesn't stir my soul. What stirs my soul and evokes national pride is our national parks, justice, equity, and people from all walks showing up fully and treating each other with dignity and care. What stirs my soul is compassion, beauty, prosperity, and fraternity. It's creativity and service. It's coming together around shared values and across differences. That is what seized me that night.

I was at a local festival called "First Friday" when Oakland's art galleries are open and the street is filled with bands, vendors, fashion shows, stand up comedy, dance troops, drum circles, political movements, spiritual communities, non-profits, and DJ booths.

In a sense, First Friday is like any street fair in the United States: folks of all ages, flirting and summer dresses, laughter and sweat, fried things on sticks. And, yet, it is like no other. Because of Oakland's diversity and culture of openness, friendships and romance flourished across lines of racial identity. Because of the Bay Area's natural beauty, public transportation, affordable healthcare, and relatively inexpensive housing, Oakland has the fertile conditions for our nation's soul to take form. How did this happen?

As technology gained a stronghold in the Bay Area during the late 1990's, rents skyrocketed, sending San Francisco's diverse artists, activists, and intellectuals to the east. Because the East Bay was separated by water and perceived to be far more dangerous and less hip than San Francisco, white yuppies largely ignored it. So, the East Bay became this little secret with incredible weather, food, music, hiking, culture, diversity, community, bike lanes, great public transit, and relatively cheap rent. Perhaps due to the progressive influence of the University of California, Berkeley, we held this Golden Age / place lightly, mindful of the numerous injustices that made it possible, from the genocide of the Ohlone and Miwok to the "Three Strikes" law that sent a generation of BIPOC folks to prison for nonviolent offenses.

Of course, now the secret is out. As a result, rents have doubled since 2012, there are Google buses and startups, Victorians are being cleared out for condos, and—because of accelerating climate change—the annual fire season turns the Bay Area into an unbreathable, post-apocalyptic hellscape.

At the time I lived there (2012-2018), however, it was magical. It seemed like everybody was up to something contributing to the common good. It felt like most folks, regardless of race or class, were actively committed to something larger than themselves. Some were involved in racial, economic, and environmental justice efforts, some were deepening their cultural traditions, some were developing their art, some were leading their Burning Man camps, some were experimenting with novel sexual endeavors and relationship statuses, some were devoted to personal and spiritual development, and some were launching community gardens, fashion brands, religions, maker spaces, intentional communities, and political movements—and some folks were like me that night, just in awe of it.

I became present to this cornucopia of brilliance that night. The magic of human creativity, flourishing, and connection, of purpose, empathy, and inclusion, interracial romance, and a sense that nothing stands in the way of our dreams. It felt like freedom in its most original and radical sense. Freedom comes from the Indo-European word, *friya*, meaning beloved, and the Old English word, *freod*, meaning affection, love, and peace. Connected and empowered, bound and creative, to be accepted wholly and completely, to claim one's destiny and to dream impossible futures. This freedom is possible when an economy and culture:

A. ensures that basic needs are secure and/or guaranteed as a right (e.g., living wages, affordable housing, healthy food, public transit, Obamacare / Covered California), and

B. makes people from all backgrounds feel safe, wanted, and empowers them to flourish.

This foundation of freedom makes it possible to pursue one's purpose. This is a freedom bound to the covenants of our unique souls. It is the freedom to be your highest self—to be the fullest expression of your unique purpose in relationship to the world. This freedom comes from connection—to your soul, your craft, your people, your earth, and the future for which you stand. It is the liberation of knowing what you are for and to whom you belong. It is the permission to care for and contribute to others, knowing that others will care for and contribute to you. It is the freedom to be wholly yourself, loving each and every one of your imperfections.

This was the freedom I experienced in the East Bay. There, it is common for folks to do inner work, have a sense of who they are and build community with others who have as well. They are cared for and connected to each other. They get wild, experiment, make mistakes, clean them up, and learn to do it better the next time.

In my time living and working among the professional class in Chicago, New York, Los Angeles, and San Francisco, I didn't observe these freedoms. I witnessed and participated in a more heartless rendering of freedom: the freedoms of detachment ("not my problem"), depersonalization ("it's just business"), dehumanization ("the world needs ditch diggers too"), and debauchery ("more of everything"). We lived from the neck up as eagles, working the angles, trading gossip on hot startups, unicorn stocks, cheap real estate, and other forms of Machiavellian comeuppance.

My experience of people living in the East Bay was radically different. There was compassion, rootedness, attachment, and connection. Folks were centered in their hearts, connected to what broke their hearts and the world they were creating. We experienced what Heather McGhee describes as a "solidarity dividend"–the prosperity and fulfillment that results from realizing our bonds to each other and working for a future that is greater than "the sum of us."

This is what it means to fulfill our national purpose. Everyone has what they need to flourish, to discover and activate their purpose, to build community with their diverse peers, and to feel safe, wanted, and connected to a larger mission. They unlock a sense of fulfillment, and belonging that they bring home to their families and communities. In so far as business is the sandbox for the activation of purpose and belonging, it is a force for the greater economic, social, environmental, cultural, and national good. In so far as it isn't, it continues to desecrate it. Let us choose the bright, connected, creative, and abundant path. Let us ignite purpose and belonging at scale.

Imagine the 20 largest employers in your area paying living wages and activating purpose and belonging in their workforce. Imagine the increase in productivity, fulfillment, inclusion, leadership effectiveness, innovation, and tenure. Imagine the resulting prosperity and tax revenues that would flow into our diverse communities. Imagine the quality of our public schools, clean energy, mass transit, and healthcare that could be available because of the expanded tax base and enhanced ability to issue municipal bonds and invest in public works. Imagine police not murdering anyone ever again, but instead, public safely is reimagined and centers mental health, de-escalation, and conflict resolution.

Imagine a deep regard and respect for all of life. Imagine enjoying soulful camaraderie, creativity, curiosity, and celebration as the foundation of our public life. Imagine engaging in intellectually sober, civil, and empathetic political discourse. Imagine our twin genocides healed and repaired. Imagine all of us sleeping well. Imagine your kids and grandkids respecting what you do for a living and seeing what you stand for in the world. Imagine all the fun possibilities now at our fingertips.

All this and more is available to you, your company, your community, and your country. We have the knowledge, tools, and resources. Help isn't coming from anywhere else. It's on us. We can and must rebuild.

When we activate PURPOSE and belonging at WORK, we become a NATION.

Stay in the conversation at http://PurposeWork.us, a community of purpose-driven leaders who support each other in building purposeful organizations and a thriving nation.

Appendix A

Purpose Activation Resources

"We cannot become ourselves by ourselves."

- Arthur Clutton-Brock

It is impossible to discover, embody, and activate one's purpose alone. I've never seen it happen. Nobody ever had an ah-ha, and then changed their life completely by themselves. Nobody ever picked up a book, did an exercise, and instantly became purpose-activated. No matter how powerful the dispatch from your soul, it cannot be activated until there is a significant measure of reflection, sharing, and integration in the key areas of life (e.g., career, love, health, home, etc.).

This is because purpose is not a piece of missing information or a problem to solve. It's not a journal exercise or a strategic plan or a 5-day challenge or an app or a matter of pure will. The brain can't figure it out because it isn't a matter of the brain. It's a revelation, and a matter of the soul that needs witnessing, nature, movement, creativity, structure, reflection, spaciousness, feedback from trusted friends and family, and really good questions.

As such, to fully activate your purpose, please explore the following approaches, by working with:

1. a trained Purpose Coach 1:1, or
2. a friend, colleague, or mentor who has completed their own purpose journey, or
3. in community with other people who are also committed to discovering and activating their purpose.

Below are some thoughts on the relative merits of these approaches.

#1 Work 1:1 with a Purpose Coach

The benefit of working with a trained Purpose Coach is that they can get you through the process more effectively and quickly, by attuning to where you are in your journey, and structuring experiences that are tailored to your development. This is especially important with respect to transforming your inner voices (e.g., inner critic, protector, etc.), who try to protect you by obscuring, resisting, and/or sabotaging your purpose.

Further, coaches frequently include a purpose integration component at the end of a program, where they empower you to activate your purpose in every area of your life. The better coaches will help you land in a soulful or purposeful community, so that you are supported ongoingly in fully activating your purpose. The best coaches offer a satisfaction guarantee, wherein they will keep working with you at no charge until you are completely satisfied. The investment is somewhere between $2-10,000 (2022 USD).

Where to find trained Purpose Coaches / Soul Guides:

- Global Purpose Leaders - http://globalpurposeleaders.org
- True Purpose Institute - http://truepurposeinstitute.com
- Animas Valley Institute - http://animas.org

- Wayfinder - http://marthabeck.com/life-coach-training/instructors

#2 Work with a friend, colleague, or mentor

The benefit of working with a friend, colleague, or mentor who has completed the purpose journey is that they can provide inspiration, reflection, accountability, and support—and often won't charge you for it. The downside is that they typically aren't able to attune to your unique development, nor skillfully help you deal with the inner voices of resistance, nor integrate your purpose into each area of your life, nor help you find / craft a purposeful community so your purpose can grow roots.

Where to find purpose discovery exercises for using with a friend, colleague, or mentor:

- *The Purpose Field Guide* by Brandon Peele
- *Finding Your Own North Star* by Martha Beck
- *True Purpose* by Tim Kelley
- *Leading From Purpose* by Nick Craig

#3 Engage in a Group Purpose Program

The benefit of engaging in a purpose program with a community of fellow participants is that you can understand a great deal about how to activate your own purpose by learning from the experiences of your peers. Also, your group will hold you accountable to complete the exercises and share what you learn so the whole group can benefit. While not as effective as working with a coach 1:1, groups can offer great support in overcoming resistance to taking purpose-aligned action. If the group is optimized for diversity, you'll also expand your understanding of people from different backgrounds and begin to touch the deeper threads of our shared humanity. After 25% of a community is purpose activated, purpose starts to become a cultural norm, wherein people are expected to fulfill their purpose, share their gifts with their community, and turn to each other for guidance. The program fees that you or your organization will pay to join a group purpose program are in the $200-4,000 / person range (2022 USD).

Where to find group purpose offerings:

- For enterprises: Unity Lab (http://unitylab.co), Imperative (http://imperative.com)
- For schools: nXu (http://nxueducation.org), Project Wayfinder (https://www.projectwayfinder.com/)
- For religious organizations: Center for Action and Contemplation (https://cac.org/)
- For individuals: Animas Valley Institute (http://animas.org)

Other Purpose Resources:

Books on purpose and soul:

- *The Golden Thread* by Holly Woods
- *Planet on Purpose* by Brandon Peele
- *Regenerative Purpose* by Wendy May
- *Nature and the Human Soul* by Bill Plotkin
- *Women Who Run with the Wolves* by Clarissa Pinkola Estes
- *Fate and Destiny* by Michael Meade
- *life re-VISION* by Anamaria Aristizabal
- *Care of the Soul* by Thomas Moore
- *Widening Circles* by Joanna Macy
- *Ritual: Power, Healing and Community* by Malidoma Patrice Somé

Where to get support in activating your organization's purpose and values:

- True Purpose Institute Consultants (https://www.truepurposeinstitute.com/level/consultant/)
- Barrett Values Centre (https://www.valuescentre.com/)
- Future Search (https://futuresearch.net/sectors/business/)

Where to get support in evolving your organization's structures and processes to support purpose and belonging:

- BCG Brighthouse (for large enterprises: https://www.thinkbrighthouse.com/)
- DPMC (for mid-sized businesses: https://www.dpmc.us/)
- Foundation for Purposeful Organizations (for SMBs: https://www.leadfrompurpose.org/)

Where to find a community of purpose-oriented professionals:

- PurposeWork.us (http://purposework.us/)
- Kindred (https://kindredmembers.com/)
- Conscious Capitalism (https://www.consciouscapitalism.org/chapters)
- Net Impact (https://www.netimpact.org/chapter-communities)

Appendix B

Social Learning Journeys

Structuring learning experiences that are <25% content and exercises and >75% action and interaction is the key to changing beliefs and behaviors. To do this, we utilize two of the most powerful liberating structures:

1. Purpose and values reflection, and
2. Sustained, substantial (>25% of a population), and safe interactions with a small group of diverse people.

Anyone can create a social learning journey. All you need is a group of people, a shared commitment, a way to create small, diverse groups of 3-6 peers, and a curriculum that invites self-reflection and discussion. As we've explored, research suggests that programs with 5-6 small, diverse group discussions are optimal. An easy way to play with this approach is to form a small diverse book club group (3-6 people) and have 6 hour-long discussions using the reflection questions at the end of each chapter of this book as a guide.

To have maximum impact on retention, productivity, innovation, organizational commitment, and information transfer, consider making social learning the centerpiece of your culture, onboarding, wellness, L&D and DEI approach, whereby your people embark on 3 journeys a year, build 3 new sets of skills and develop 9 new diverse relationships. This is especially important for new hires, new leaders, diverse employees, and employees from newly acquired companies. So, what journeys make the most sense to enroll your teams in?

As we've explored, activating employee purpose is one of the most liberating and rewarding journeys for both the individual and organization. Once purpose is activated, future programs and skills can be delivered in a way that is personally meaningful and organizationally impactful.

For example, Unity Lab's core programs follow a progression of developing purposeful employees, then teams, and then leaders. The first two journeys—C3, and VAP—empower your people to activate their purpose and align it with the organization's mission and values. The next two—TCP and EIA—activate healthy team communication. The last program, PLA, builds the foundation of purpose-driven leadership.

1. **C3 - Clarity, Contribution, Community:** Employees activate their purpose on the job.
2. **VAP - Values Activation Program:** After activating their unique purpose and values, employees find their unique connection to the organization's mission and values.
3. **TCP - Team Communication Program:** Once clear on who they are and how their role and contribution at the company is an expression of who they are, team members develop critical team and communication skills such as active listening, gratitude, effective apologies, and "I" statements.
4. **EIA - Emotional Intelligence Accelerator:** Now that people are activated, aligned, and empowered, they take their team skills to the next level by developing the 5 key EQ skills (self-awareness, self-regulation, motivation, empathy, and social attunement).

5. **PLA - Purposeful Leader Accelerator:** With the skills to express their purpose and attune to their teams, they then are ready to begin their journey as a leader by developing the 5 key practices of purposeful leadership:
   a. model their purpose with stories and vulnerability,
   b. activate authentic connection and trust between team members,
   c. contextualize contribution,
   d. align learning, contribution, and connection goals, and
   e. sponsor diverse team members.

Once this foundation is complete, organizations can develop other critical power skills via this method, such as integrative self-care, conflict resolution, creative intelligence, cultural intelligence, storytelling, boundary setting, and persuasion.

Endnotes

In the spirit of removing *bullshit*, making the source material easy to explore, and the likelihood that you'll be engaging with this book in an e-book format and/or begin exploring online, all the sources cited below (books, articles, studies, etc.) follow the same simplified format: author last name, author first initial, *title*, source/publisher, accessed/publish date, link.

Author's Notes
1. Global Purpose Leaders, *Home page*, Accessed 5/13/2021, http://globalpurposeleaders.org/.
2. Crossley-Baxter, L., *The Welsh Word You Can't Translate*, BBC.com, 2/15/2021, http://www.bbc.com/travel/story/20210214-the-welsh-word-you-cant-translate.
3. Loprinzi, P., Branscum, A., *Mayo Clinic Proceedings*, Volume 91, Issue 4, p. 432-442, 4/1/2016, https://www.mayoclinicproceedings.org/article/S0025-6196(16)00043-4/fulltext.
4. American Psychological Association, *Stress in America™: January 2021 Stress Snapshot*, https://www.apa.org/news/press/releases/2021/02/adults-stress-pandemic.
5. Cigna, *Cigna 2020 Loneliness Index*,1/23/2020, https://newsroom.cigna.com/cigna-takes-action-to-combat-the-rise-of-loneliness-and-improve-mental-wellness-in-america.
6. Gallup, *State of the Global Workplace Report*, 2021, https://advise.gallup.com/state-of-the-global-workplace-2021.
7. Geewax, M., *Most Americans Are No Longer Middle Class*, NPR.org, 12/10/2015, https://livingwage.mit.edu/articles/13-the-tipping-point-most-americans-no-longer-are-middle-class.
8. Percheski, C., Gibbon-Davis, C., *A Penny on the Dollar: Racial Inequalities in Wealth among Households with Children*, Socius: Sociological Research for a Dynamic World, 6/1/2020, https://journals.sagepub.com/doi/full/10.1177/2378023120916616.
9. Cox, D., *After the ballots are counted: Conspiracies, political violence, and American exceptionalism*, January 2021 American Perspectives Survey, https://www.americansurveycenter.org/research/after-the-ballots-are-counted-conspiracies-political-violence-and-american-exceptionalism/.
10. Marcus, L., *Is the American Dream over? Here's what the data says,* World Economic Forum, 9/2/2020, https://www.weforum.org/agenda/2020/09/social-mobility-upwards-decline-usa-us-america-economics/.
11. MIT Living Wage Calculator, Accessed 11/4/2021, https://livingwage.mit.edu/counties/06073.
12. Leonard, A., *The Hourglass Economy*, Salon, 9/13/2011, https://www.salon.com/2011/09/13/the_hourglass_economy/.

13. Workers World, *International Tribunal finds U.S. guilty of crimes against humanity*, 11/1/2021, https://www.workers.org/2021/11/59858/?fbclid=IwAR1GNoPfLs6K_yzyoFl-t5ObCF4_i5cT8eLlo1DYwu_U_iHFg-VvJKQZZL4.

14. Edsall, T., *Trumpism Without Borders*, New York Times, 6/16/2021, https://www.nytimes.com/2021/06/16/opinion/trump-global-populism.html.

15. V-Dem Institute, *Democracy Report 2021*, March 2021 https://www.v-dem.net/democracy_reports.html.

16. Harter, J., Gallup, *U.S. Employee Engagement Holds Steady in First Half of 2021*, 7/29/2021, https://www.gallup.com/workplace/352949/employee-engagement-holds-steady-first-half-2021.aspx.

Introduction

1. Kaur, H., *About 93% of racial justice protests in the US have been peaceful, a new report finds*, CNN.com, 9/4/2020, https://www.cnn.com/2020/09/04/us/blm-protests-peaceful-report-trnd/index.html.

2. Center for Talent Innovation, *What Do White Men Really Think About Diversity and Inclusion in the Workplace?*, Cision PR Newswire, 8/4/2020, https://www.prnewswire.com/news-releases/what-do-white-men-really-think-about-diversity-and-inclusion-in-the-workplace-301104952.html.

3. Dobbin, F., Kalev, A., *Why Diversity Programs Fail*, Harvard Business Review, July 2016, https://hbr.org/2016/07/why-diversity-programs-fail.

4. McKinsey & Co., *Focusing on what works for workplace diversity*, 4/7/2017, https://www.mckinsey.com/featured-insights/gender-equality/focusing-on-what-works-for-workplace-diversity.

5. Kaiser, C., Miller, C., *Stop Complaining! The Social Costs of Making Attributions to Discrimination*, Personality and Social Psychology Bulletin, 2/1/2001, https://journals.sagepub.com/doi/abs/10.1177/0146167201272010.

6. Barton, B., Quiring, K., et al, *From me to we: The rise of the purpose-led brand*, Accenture, 12/5/18, https://www.accenture.com/us-en/insights/strategy/brand-purpose?c=strat_competitiveagilnovalue_10437227&n=mrl_1118.

7. Edelman, *2017 Edelman Trust Barometer*, 1/21/2017, https://www.edelman.com/trust/2017-trust-barometer.

8. Peele, B., Asbaty, C., *The Impact of Small Group Discussions on Behavior Change, Retention, and Trust in Large Enterprises*, 10/1/2020, https://www.ionlearning.com/social-learning-study.

9. Jordan, K., *MOOC Completion Rates: The Data*, 6/12/15, http://www.katyjordan.com/MOOCproject.html.

10. Mankins, M., Garton, E., *Time, Talent, Energy: Overcome Organizational Drag and Unleash Your Team's Productive Power*, Harvard Business Review, 3/7/2017, https://store.hbr.org/product/time-talent-energy-overcome-organizational-drag-and-unleash-your-team-s-productive-power/10031?sku=10031-HBK-ENG.

11. Anderson R., Adams, W., *Mastering Leadership*, Wiley, 11/30/2015, https://smile.amazon.com/dp/B015EN6NXK/ref=dp-kindle-redirect?_encoding=UTF8&btkr=1.

12. O'Brien, D., Main, A., et al, *2020 Global Marketing Trends*, Deloitte, 2020, https://www2.deloitte.com/content/dam/insights/us/articles/2020-global-marketing-trends/DI_2020%20Global%20Marketing%20Trends.pdf

13. Burrows, A., Hill, P., *Derailed by Diversity? Purpose Buffers the Relationship Between Ethnic Composition on Trains and Passenger Negative Mood*, Personality and Social Psychology Bulletin, 8/17/2013, https://journals.sagepub.com/doi/abs/10.1177/0146167213499377.

14. Reese, A., Kellerman, G., *Latest Research on Meaning and Purpose at Work*, BetterUp, 2019, https://grow.betterup.com/resources/meaning-and-purpose-report.

Chapter 1

1. Bureau of Labor Statistics, *Median usual weekly earnings of full-time wage and salary workers by age, race, Hispanic or Latino ethnicity, and sex, fourth quarter 2021 averages, not seasonally adjusted*, Accessed October 19, 2021, https://www.bls.gov/news.release/wkyeng.t03.htm

2. Census.gov, *Work Experience-People 15 Years Old and Over, by Total Money Earnings, Age, Race, Hispanic Origin, Sex, and Disability Status*, October 8, 2021, https://www.census.gov/data/tables/time-series/demo/income-poverty/cps-pinc/pinc-05.html.

3. Percheski, C., Gibson-Davis, C., *A Penny on the Dollar: Racial Inequalities in Wealth among Households with Children*, Socius: Sociological Research for a Dynamic World, 6/1/2020, https://journals.sagepub.com/doi/full/10.1177/2378023120916616.

4. Charlesworth, T., Banaji, M., *Patterns of Implicit and Explicit Attitudes: I. Long-Term Change and Stability From 2007 to 2016*, Association for Psychological Science, 1/23/2019, https://journals.sagepub.com/doi/abs/10.1177/0956797618813087?journalCode=pssa.

5. Zinn, H., *A People's History of the United States*, Bello, 2016, https://smile.amazon.com/dp/B01BBHZMJO/ref=dp-kindle-redirect?_encoding=UTF8&btkr=1.

6. Dunbar-Ortiz, R., *An Indigenous People's History of the United States*, Beacon Press, 2014, https://smile.amazon.com/Indigenous-Peoples-History-ReVisioning-American-ebook/dp/B00J6Y98UE/ref=sr_1_1?keywords=an+indigenous+peoples%27+history+of+the+united+states&qid=1644510427&s=digital-text&sprefix=an+indig%2Cdigital-text%2C160&sr=1-1.

7. Hannah-Jones, N., *The 1619 Project: A New Origin Story*, One World, 2021, https://smile.amazon.com/1619-Project-New-Origin-Story-ebook/dp/B08XYPW4G7/ref=sr_1_3?keywords=1619+project&qid=1644510554&s=digital-text&sprefix=1619%2Cdigital-text%2C246&sr=1-3.

8. Stone Brown, S., *Native Self-Actualization*, 2014, BookPatch, https://app.thebookpatch.com/BookStore/transformation-beyond-greed/7c35ed9c-d2ee-4b79-a036-455daa34669e?isbn=9781633183636.

9. Heard, J.N., *The Assimilation of Captives on the American Frontier in the Eighteenth and Nineteenth Centuries*, Louisiana State University, 1977, https://digitalcommons.lsu.edu/cgi/viewcontent.cgi?article=4156&context=gradschool_disstheses.

10. Franklin, B., *From Benjamin Franklin to Peter Collinson, 9 May 1753*, National Archivs, 1753, ,https://founders.archives.gov/documents/Franklin/01-04-02-0173.

11. Graeber, D., Wengrow, D., *The Dawn of Everything: A New History of Humanity*, Farrar, Straus, Giroux, 2021, https://us.macmillan.com/books/9780374157357/thedawnofeverything.

12. Ibid.

13. O'Neil, A., *Black and slave population of the United States from 1790 to 1880*, Statista.com, 2021, https://www.statista.com/statistics/1010169/black-and-slave-population-us-1790-1880/.

14. Fogel, R., *Time on the Cross: The Economics of American Slavery*. Little, Brown and Company. p. 125., 1974, https://smile.amazon.com/Time-Cross-Economics-American-Slavery/dp/0393312186.

15. Norton, Q., *How White People Got Made*, Medium.com, 10/17/2014, https://medium.com/message/how-white-people-got-made-6eeb076ade42.

16. Equal Justice Initiative, *The Legacy Museum*, Accessed August, 2021, https://museumandmemorial.eji.org/museum.

17. Wikipedia, *United States involvement in regime change*, Accessed 1/3/2021, https://en.wikipedia.org/wiki/United_States_involvement_in_regime_change

18. Packer, G., *HOW AMERICA FRACTURED INTO FOUR PARTS*, The Atlantic, July, 2021, https://www.theatlantic.com/magazine/archive/2021/07/george-packer-four-americas/619012/.

19. Purdue Global, *Generational Differences in the Workplace*, Accessed 7/8/2021, https://www.purdueglobal.edu/education-partnerships/generational-workforce-differences-infographic/.

20. Barna, *U.S. Adults Have Few Friends—and They're Mostly Alike*, Barna.com, 10/23/2018, https://www.barna.com/research/friends-loneliness/.

21. Cox, D., Streeter, R. et al, *Socially distant: How our divided social networks explain our politics*, Survey Center on American Life, 9/23/2020, https://www.americansurveycenter.org/research/socially-distant-how-our-divided-social-networks-explain-our-politics/.

22. Bresler, J., Wexler, E. et al, *The Return of School Segregation in Eight Charts*, 7/15/2014, https://www.pbs.org/wgbh/frontline/article/the-return-of-school-segregation-in-eight-charts/.

23. Mervosh, S., *How Much Wealthier Are White School Districts Than Nonwhite Ones? $23 Billion, Report Says*, New York Times, 2/27/2019, https://www.nytimes.com/2019/02/27/education/school-districts-funding-white-minorities.html.

24. Steimer, S., *Insurrectionist movement in U.S. is larger and more dangerous than expected, research finds*, UChicago News, 8/12/2021, https://news.uchicago.edu/story/insurrectionist-movement-us-larger-and-more-dangerous-expected-research-finds.

25. DiAngelo, R., *No, I Won't Stop Saying "White Supremacy"*, Yes! Magazine, 6/30/2107, https://www.yesmagazine.org/democracy/2017/06/30/no-i-wont-stop-saying-white-supremacy.

26. Stout, D., *Dismayed Greenwich Confronts a Message of Hate in a Yearbook*, New York Times, 6/15/1995, https://www.nytimes.com/1995/06/15/nyregion/dismayed-greenwich-confronts-a-message-of-hate-in-a-yearbook.html.

27. Korn, S., *When No Means Yes*, The Harvard Crimson, 11/12/2010, https://www.thecrimson.com/article/2010/11/12/yale-dke-harvard-womens/.

28. Sganga, N. *What to know about the civil trial over Charlottesville's deadly "Unite the Right" rally*, CBS News, 11/19/2021, https://www.cbsnews.com/news/charlottesville-unite-the-right-rally-trial-what-to-know/

29. Think, *How Schools Are Funneling Black Students Into The Prison System*, NBC News, 6/15/2020, https://www.youtube.com/watch?v=QZsgk9acYbo.

30. Putnam, R., Garret, S., *The Upswing*, Simon & Schuster, 2021, https://www.simonandschuster.com/books/The-Upswing/Robert-D-Putnam/9781982129156.

31. Waskow, D., Gerholdt, R., *5 Big Findings from the IPCC's 2021 Climate Report*, World Resources Institute, 8/09/2021, https://www.wri.org/insights/ipcc-climate-report.

32. Akala, A., *Cost Of Racism: U.S. Economy Lost $16 Trillion Because Of Discrimination, Bank Says*, NPR, 9/23/2020, https://www.npr.org/sections/live-updates-protests-for-racial-justice/2020/09/23/916022472/cost-of-racism-u-s-economy-lost-16-trillion-because-of-discrimination-bank-says.

33. MIT, *Living Wage Calculator*, 2021, https://livingwage.mit.edu/.

34. Jones, J., *U.S. Church Membership Falls Below Majority for First Time*, Gallup, 3/29/2021, https://news.gallup.com/poll/341963/church-membership-falls-below-majority-first-time.aspx.

35. Cigna, *Cigna Takes Action To Combat The Rise Of Loneliness And Improve Mental Wellness In America*, Cigna.com, 1/23/2020, https://newsroom.cigna.com/cigna-takes-action-to-combat-the-rise-of-loneliness-and-improve-mental-wellness-in-america.

36. Cox, D., Streeter R., et al, *Socially distant: How our divided social networks explain our politics*, Survey Center on American Life, 9/30/2020, https://www.americansurveycenter.org/research/socially-distant-how-our-divided-social-networks-explain-our-politics/.

37. Cox, D., *The state of American friendship: Change, challenges, and loss*, Survey Center on American Life, 6/8/2021, https://www.americansurveycenter.org/research/the-state-of-american-friendship-change-challenges-and-loss/.

38. Vallier, K., *US Social Trust Has Fallen 23 Points Since 1964*, Kevinvallier.com, 11/30/2020, https://www.kevinvallier.com/reconciled/new-finding-us-social-trust-has-fallen-23-points-since-1964/.

39. Cox, D., Streeter R., et al, *Socially distant: How our divided social networks explain our politics*, Survey Center on American Life, 9/30/2020, https://www.americansurveycenter.org/research/socially-distant-how-our-divided-social-networks-explain-our-politics/.

40. Provine, R., Fisher, K., *Laughing, Smiling, and Talking: Relation to Sleeping and Social Context in Humans*, Ethology, Volume 3, Issue 4, December-January 1989, https://onlinelibrary.wiley.com/doi/abs/10.1111/j.1439-0310.1989.tb00536.x?casa_token=CKDdALCRS18AAAAA:Bv2j_Lf6Gs8TeNX-xHf7XVjXqBdeIOcJb3sQ_bBMKsr-DTVaFq-jz77z8SZhNDrAttJ3zMK-jf0cwl8.

41. Watts, E., *Depression rates in the US more than tripled during the pandemic*, Medical News Today, 10/11/2021, https://www.medicalnewstoday.com/articles/depression-rates-in-the-us-more-than-tripled-during-the-pandemic#Study-shows-depression-increase.

42. Moore, T., Mattison, D., *Adult Utilization of Psychiatric Drugs and Differences by Sex, Age, and Race*, JAMA Intern Med, 2017 Feb 1;177(2):274-275 https://pubmed.ncbi.nlm.nih.gov/27942726/.

43. Twenge, J., *Generation Me*, Atria Books, 9/13/2014, https://www.amazon.com/Generation-Americans-Confident-Assertive-Entitled/dp/1476755566.

44. Ortiz-Ospina, E., Roser, M., *Trust*, OurWorldInData.org, 2016, https://ourworldindata.org/trust.

45. American Academy of Pediatrics, *AAP, AACAP, CHA declare national emergency in children's mental health*, AAP.org, October 19, 2021, https://publications.aap.org/aapnews/news/17718.

46. Desilver, D., *For most U.S. workers, real wages have barely budged in decades*, Pew Research Center, 8/7/2018, https://www.pewresearch.org/fact-tank/2018/08/07/for-most-us-workers-real-wages-have-barely-budged-for-decades/.

47. Gilens, M. Page, B., *Testing Theories of American Politics: Elites, Interest Groups, and Average Citizens*, American Political Science Association, 2014 https://scholar.princeton.edu/sites/default/files/mgilens/files/gilens_and_page_2014_-testing_theories_of_american_politics.doc.pdf.

48. Hanauer, N., Rolf, D., *The Top 1% of Americans Have Taken $50 Trillion From the Bottom 90%—And That's Made the U.S. Less Secure*, Time.com, 9/14/2020, https://time.com/5888024/50-trillion-income-inequality-america/.

49. Cubias, D., *Solidarity Dividend: A New Way to Fight Racism?*, Mano Magazine, 5/10/2021, https://manomagazine.com/politics-racism-heather-mcghee-daniel-cubias-solidarity-dividend/.

50. Protect Democracy, *Democracy Crisis in the Making: Year-end Report Update*, December, 2021, https://protectdemocracy.org/project/democracy-crisis-in-the-making/#section-3.

51. Pew Research Center, *Public Trust in Government: 1958-2021*, 2021, https://www.pewresearch.org/politics/2021/05/17/public-trust-in-government-1958-2021/.

52. Cox, D., *After the ballots are counted: Conspiracies, political violence, and American exceptionalism*, Survey Center on American Life, 2/11/2021, https://www.americansurveycenter.org/research/after-the-ballots-are-counted-conspiracies-political-violence-and-american-exceptionalism/.

53. Mansfield, M., *DREAM IS OVER Most in US say 'the American dream' is dead*, The Sun, 11/12/2020, https://www.the-sun.com/news/1789405/american-dream-over-survey/.

54. Friedman, T., *How to Stop Trump and Prevent Another Jan. 6*, New York Times, 1/4/2022, https://www.nytimes.com/2022/01/04/opinion/trump-jan-6-democracy.html.

55. Centola, D., *Change*, Little, Brown, Spark, 2021, https://www.amazon.com/dp/B0859TZWVG/ref=dp-kindle-redirect?_encoding=UTF8&btkr=1.

56. Ibid.

57. Gallup, *Confidence in Institutions*, 2021, https://news.gallup.com/poll/1597/confidence-institutions.aspx.

58. U.S. Small Business Administration, *Frequently Asked Questions*, SBA.gov, December 2021, https://cdn.advocacy.sba.gov/wp-content/uploads/2021/12/06095731/Small-Business-FAQ-Revised-December-2021.pdf.

59. Edelman, *Edelman Trust Barometer 2021*, 2021 https://www.edelman.com/sites/g/files/aatuss191/files/2021-08/2021EdelmanTrustBarometerSpecialReport_TheBelief-DrivenEmployee.pdf.

60. Ibid.

61. Dingra, N., Samo, A., et al, *Help your employees find purpose—or watch them leave*, McKinsey & Co. 4/5/2021, https://www.mckinsey.com/business-functions/people-and-organizational-performance/our-insights/help-your-employees-find-purpose-or-watch-them-leave.

62. Hurst, A., *2019 Workforce Purpose Index*, Imperative, 2019, https://www.imperative.com/2019wpi.

63. Beroe, Inc., *L&D Industry to Touch $402 Billion Mark by 2025*, Says Beroe Inc, 4/22/2021, https://www.prnewswire.com/news-releases/ld-industry-to-touch-402-billion-mark-by-2025-says-beroe-inc-301274531.html.

64. Kirkland, R., Bohnet, I., *Focusing on what works for workplace diversity*, McKinsey & Co., 4/7/2017, https://www.mckinsey.com/featured-insights/gender-equality/focusing-on-what-works-for-workplace-diversity.

65. Globe News Wire, 7/29/2021, *Global Corporate Wellness Market to Reach $87.3 Billion by 2026*, https://www.globenewswire.com/news-release/2021/07/29/2270961/0/en/Global-Corporate-Wellness-Market-to-Reach-87-3-Billion-by-2026.html.

Chapter 2

1. Stamp, J., *American Myths: Benjamin Franklin's Turkey and the Presidential Seal*, Smithsonianmag.com, 1/25/2013, https://www.smithsonianmag.com/arts-culture/american-myths-benjamin-franklins-turkey-and-the-presidential-seal-6623414/.

2. Abdelfatah, R., Arablouie, R., et al, *Capitalism: God Wants You To Be Rich*, NPR Throughline, 7/8/2021, https://www.npr.org/2021/07/06/1013430166/capitalism-god-wants-you-to-be-rich.

3. Graeber, D., *Bullshit Jobs: A Theory*, Simon & Schuster, 2018, https://smile.amazon.com/Bullshit-Jobs-Theory-David-Graeber-ebook/dp/B075RWG7YM/ref=sr_1_1?crid=HZOSLVDDTT7Y&keywords=bullshit+jobs&qid=1644512242&s=digital-text&sprefix=bullshit+job%2Cdigital-text%2C166&sr=1-1.

4. Curtis, A., *The Century of the Self*, BBC Two England, March, 24, 2002https://www.youtube.com/watch?v=eJ3RzGoQC4s.

5. KesebirP., Kesebir, S., *The Cultural Salience of Moral Character and Virtue Declined in Twentieth Century America*, The Journal of Positive Psychology, 7:6, 471-480, 5/14/2012, https://www.tandfonline.com/doi/abs/10.1080/17439760.2012.715182

6. Twenge, J., *Generation Me*, Atria Books, 9/13/2014, https://www.amazon.com/Generation-Americans-Confident-Assertive-Entitled/dp/1476755566.

7. Konrath, S., O'Brien, E., et al, *Changes in Dispositional Empathy in American College Students Over Time: A Meta-Analysis*, Personality and Social Psychology Review, Volume: 15 issue: 2, page(s): 180-198, August 5, 2010, https://journals.sagepub.com/doi/abs/10.1177/1088868310377395.

8. McIntyre, G., *What Percentage of Small Businesses Fail? (And Other Need-to-Know Stats)*, Fundera.com, 11/20/2020, https://www.fundera.com/blog/what-percentage-of-small-businesses-fail.

9. Steinbeck, J., Goodreads.com, Accessed 1/4/2022, https://www.goodreads.com/quotes/7234438-except-for-the-field-organizers-of-strikes-who-were-pretty.

10. Maslin Nir, S., *A Fourth of July Symbol of Unity That May No Longer Unite*, New York Times, 7/3/2021, https://www.nytimes.com/2021/07/03/nyregion/american-flag-politics-polarization.html.

11. National Park Service, *Bison Bellows: America's New National Mammal*, NPS.ogv, Accessed 1/5/2022, https://www.nps.gov/articles/bison-bellows-5-12-16.htm.

12. de Waal, Frans ,*The Age of Empathy: Nature's Lessons for a Kinder Society*, Crown, 2010, https://www.amazon.com/dp/B002PYFW8Y/ref=dp-kindle-redirect?_encoding=UTF8&btkr=1.

13. Thomsello, M., Dweck, C. *Why We Cooperate*, MIT Press, 2009, https://mitpress.mit.edu/books/why-we-cooperate#:~:text=They%20become%20more%20aware%20of,of%20innate%20and%20learned%20behavior.

14. CDC, *What is epigenetics?*, CDC.gov, Accessed 1/5/2022, https://www.cdc.gov/genomics/disease/epigenetics.htm#:~:text=Epigenetics%20is%20the%20study%20of,body%20reads%20a%20DNA%20sequence.

15. Maine Beer Company, *Employment*, Mainebeercompany.com, accessed 1/5/2022, https://mainebeercompany.com/employment

16. BetterUp, *The Value of Belonging at Work: New Frontiers for Inclusion in 2021 and Beyond*, Betterup.com, 2021, https://grow.betterup.com/resources/the-value-of-belonging-at-work-the-business-case-for-investing-in-workplace-inclusion.

17. BetterUp, *Latest Research on Meaning and Purpose At Work*, Betterup, 2019, https://grow.betterup.com/resources/meaning-and-purpose-report.

18. Sperry, K., *Ethics + Stakeholder Focus = Greater Long-Run Shareholder Profits*, Torrey Project, 4/6/2020, https://www.torreyproject.org/post/ethics-stakeholder-focus-greater-long-run-shareholder-profits.

19. Feldman, J., *Purpose Powered Success*, Korn Ferry, 2016, https://www.kornferry.com/insights/this-week-in-leadership/purpose-powered-success.

20. Kotter, J., Haskett, J., *Corporate Culture Performance*, Free Press, 2011 https://www.amazon.com/Corporate-Culture-Performance-John-Kotter/dp/1451655320.

21. Zeno Group, *The 2020 Zeno Strength of Purpose Study*, 6/17/2020, https://www.zenogroup.com/insights/2020-zeno-strength-purpose.

22. Cone / Porter Novelli, *2018 CONE/PORTER NOVELLI PURPOSE STUDY*, 2018, https://www.conecomm.com/research-blog/2018-purpose-study#download-the-research.

23. Edelman, *2017 Edelman Trust Barometer*, 2017 https://www.edelman.com/trust/2017-trust-barometer.

24. Fuse, *Your Future Consumer's Views on Social Activism and Cause Marketing and How It Differs from What Millennials Think*, Fusemarketing.com, October, 2105, https://www.fusemarketing.com/thought-leadership/future-consumers-views-cause-marketing-social-activism/.

25. Kapner, S., Chinni, D., *Are Your Jeans Red or Blue? Shopping America's Partisan Divide,* Wall Street Journal, 11/19/2019, https://www.wsj.com/articles/are-your-jeans-red-or-blue-shopping-americas-partisan-divide-11574185777.

26. Mankin, M., Gartner, F., *Time, Talent, Energy: Overcome Organizational Drag and Unleash Your Team's Productive Power*, Harvard Business Review Press, 2017, https://www.amazon.com/Time-Talent-Energy-Organizational-Productive-ebook/dp/B01LBRS42G.

27. Harris Poll / Kumanu, *Harris-Kumanu Purpose Index*, Kumanu.com, 2021, https://www.kumanu.com/dignity-and-purpose-in-a-pandemic/.

28. Feldman, J., *Purpose Powered Success*, Korn Ferry, 2016, https://www.kornferry.com/insights/this-week-in-leadership/purpose-powered-success.

29. Gallup, *State of the Global Workplace 2021 Report*, 2021, https://www.gallup.com/workplace/349484/state-of-the-global-workplace.aspx.

30. Energy Project, *The Human Era @ Work*, Harvard Business Review, 2014, https://uli.org/wp-content/uploads/ULI-Documents/The-Human-Era-at-Work.pdf.

Chapter 3

1. Horowitz, J., *Support for Black Lives Matter declined after George Floyd protests, but has remained unchanged since*, Pew Research Center, 9/27/2021, https://www.pewresearch.org/fact-tank/2021/09/27/support-for-black-lives-matter-declined-after-george-floyd-protests-but-has-remained-unchanged-since/.

2. Cox, D., Streeter, R. et al, *Socially distant: How our divided social networks explain our politics*, Survey Center on American Life, 9/30/2020, https://www.americansurveycenter.org/research/socially-distant-how-our-divided-social-networks-explain-our-politics/.

3. Salvanto, A., Khanna, K. et al, *Americans see democracy under threat — CBS News poll*, CBS News, 1/27/2021, https://www.cbsnews.com/news/joe-biden-coronavirus-opinion-poll/.

4. Cox, D., *After the ballots are counted: Conspiracies, political violence, and American exceptionalism*, Survey Center on American Life, 2/11/2021, https://www.americansurveycenter.org/research/after-the-ballots-are-counted-conspiracies-political-violence-and-american-exceptionalism/.

5. Kalmoe, N., Mason, L., *Lethal Mass Partisanship*, Dannyhayes.org, 2019, https://www.dannyhayes.org/uploads/6/9/8/5/69858539/kalmoe___mason_ncapsa_2019_-_lethal_partisanship_-_final_lmedit.pdf.

6. Black Lives Matter, *About*, Blacklivesmatter.com, accessed 2/7/2022, https://blacklivesmatter.com/about/.

7. Beinhart, P., *Trump Shut Programs to Counter Violent Extremism*, The Atlantic, 10/29/18, https://www.theatlantic.com/ideas/archive/2018/10/trump-shut-countering-violent-extremism-program/574237/.

8. Hall, L., *'Creepy' blue dots painted outside homes of Biden supporters in California*, Independent,11/03/2020, https://www.independent.co.uk/news/world/americas/us-election-2020/creepy-blue-dots-spraypaint-homes-biden-b1561327.html?fbclid=IwAR0AT31xNiCmLfuRG54yXJLCYSnuptKmYO1nyCEvgcaGt86xGrv4Sxs_qc0.

9. Arango, T., Abi-Habib, M., *In California, Hanging Deaths of Two Black Men Summon a Dark History and F.B.I. Scrutiny*, New York Times, 6/21/2020, https://www.nytimes.com/2020/06/19/us/hanging-deaths-california.html.

10. Alba, D., *Nooses, Anger and No Answers: Inside the Uproar Over a Future Amazon Site*, New York Times, 7/30/2021, https://www.nytimes.com/2021/07/30/technology/amazon-nooses-warehouse.html.

11. Salvanto, A., Khanna, K. et al, *Americans see democracy under threat — CBS News poll*, CBS News, 1/27/2021, https://www.cbsnews.com/news/joe-biden-coronavirus-opinion-poll/.

12. Ibid.

13. Weber Shandwick, Powell Tate & KRC Research, *Civility in America 2019*, Webershandwick.com, 2019, https://www.webershandwick.com/wp-content/uploads/2019/06/CivilityInAmerica2019SolutionsforTomorrow.pdf.

14. Kagan, R., *Our constitutional crisis is already here*, Washington Post, 9/23/2021, https://www.washingtonpost.com/opinions/2021/09/23/robert-kagan-constitutional-crisis/?fbclid=IwAR2_kXb-qwXcUpXw6M3L8xNvUl09Xj1IkCskauBLgH_8_7Umopbqo5jpUeE.

15. Klawans, J., *82% of Fox News, 97% of OANN, Newsmax Viewers Believe Trump's Stolen Election Claim: Poll*, Newsweek, 11/01/2021, https://www.newsweek.com/82-fox-news-97-oann-newsmax-viewers-believe-trumps-stolen-election-claim-poll-1644756.

16. Lerer, L., Herndon, A., *Menace Enters the Republican Mainstream*, New York Times, 11/16/2021, https://www.nytimes.com/2021/11/12/us/politics/republican-violent-rhetoric.html.

17. Karp, A., *Estimating Global CivilianHELD Firearms Numbers*, Small Arms Survey, June 2018, https://www.smallarmssurvey.org/sites/default/files/resources/SAS-BP-Civilian-Firearms-Numbers.pdf.

18. Steimer, S., *Insurrectionist movement in U.S. is larger and more dangerous than expected, research finds*, UChicago News, 8/12/2021, https://news.uchicago.edu/story/insurrectionist-movement-us-larger-and-more-dangerous-expected-research-finds.

19. Southern Poverty Law Center, *Hate Map*, Splcenter.org, 2020, https://www.splcenter.org/hate-map.

20. Ekins, E., *Poll: 62% of Americans Say They Have Political Views They're Afraid to Share*, Cato Institute, 7/22/2020, https://www.cato.org/survey-reports/poll-62-americans-say-they-have-political-views-theyre-afraid-share.

21. Porter, M., Rivkin, J. et al, *Report: Pessimism about the Future of the U.S. Economy Deepens; Political Dysfunction the Greatest Barrier to Strengthening U.S. Competitiveness*, Harvard Business School, 9/15/2016, https://www.hbs.edu/news/releases/Pages/fifth-us-competitiveness-assessment.aspx.

22. Smith, R., *Design Your Culture, Apollo 13 Style*, A Human Workplace, 8/31/2021, https://www.makeworkmorehuman.com/blog/design-your-culture-apollo-13-styl.

23. Riley, T., *Just 100 companies responsible for 71% of global emissions, study says*, The Guardian, 7/10/2017, https://www.theguardian.com/sustainable-business/2017/jul/10/100-fossil-fuel-companies-investors-responsible-71-global-emissions-cdp-study-climate-change.

Chapter 4

1. Center for Talent Innovation, *What Do White Men Really Think About Diversity and Inclusion in the Workplace?*, PR Newswire, 8/04/2020, https://www.prnewswire.com/news-releases/what-do-white-men-really-think-about-diversity-and-inclusion-in-the-workplace-301104952.html.

2. Edelman, Edelman Trust Barometer 2021, Edelman.com, 2021, https://www.edelman.com/sites/g/files/aatuss191/files/2021-08/2021EdelmanTrustBarometerSpecialReport_TheBelief-DrivenEmployee.pdf.

3. Centola, D., *Change*, Little, Brown, Spark, 2021, https://www.amazon.com/dp/B0859TZWVG/ref=dp-kindle-redirect?_encoding=UTF8&btkr=1.

4. Thomas, D., Horowitz, J.M., *Support for Black Lives Matter has decreased since June but remains strong among Black Americans*, Pew Research Center, 9/16/2020, https://www.pewresearch.org/fact-tank/2020/09/16/support-for-black-lives-matter-has-decreased-since-june-but-remains-strong-among-black-americans/.

5. Edgecliffe-Johnson, A., Rogers, T., *Are CEOs living up to the pledges they made after George Floyd's murder?*, Financial Times, 5/5/2021, https://www.ft.com/content/67e79b20-bc41-4cb0-992f-a28e3eaa5695.

6. Armstrong, K., *'I Feel Your Pain': The Neuroscience of Empathy*, Association for Psychological Science, 12/29/2017, https://www.psychologicalscience.org/observer/neuroscience-empathy.

7. Jacquet, R., *Upskilling During Difficult Times: How Do We Keep Employees Learning from Home?*, Courserian, 7/20/2020, https://the-courserian-blog.mystagingwebsite.com/upskilling-during-difficult-times-how-do-we-keep-employees-learning-from-home.

8. Mastroianni, B., *How Climate Change Disproportionately Affects People of Color*, Healthline, 4/22/2021, https://www.healthline.com/health-news/how-climate-change-disproportionately-affects-people-of-color.

9. Centers for Disease Control and Prevention, *Racism is a Serious Threat to the Public's Health*, Accessed 1/29/2021, https://www.cdc.gov/healthequity/racism-disparities/index.html.

10. Murre, J., Dros, J., *Replication and Analysis of Ebbinghaus' Forgetting Curve*, PLoS One, 7/6/2015, https://www.ncbi.nlm.nih.gov/pmc/articles/PMC4492928/.

11. Beroe, Inc., *L&D Industry to Touch $402 Billion Mark by 2025*, Says Beroe Inc, 4/22/2021, PR Newswire, https://www.prnewswire.com/news-releases/ld-industry-to-touch-402-billion-mark-by-2025-says-beroe-inc-301274531.html.

12. Gore H., *Action-based learning with myQuest*, myQuest, 4/15/2019, https://www.myquest.co/blog/action-based-learning.

13. Dasgupta, N., Greenwald, A., *On the malleability of automatic attitudes: combating automatic prejudice with images of admired and disliked individuals*, J Pers Soc Psychol. 2001 Nov, 81(5):800-14, https://pubmed.ncbi.nlm.nih.gov/11708558/

14. Saletan, W., *Why Won't They Listen?*, New York Times, 3/23/2012, https://www.nytimes.com/2012/03/25/books/review/the-righteous-mind-by-jonathan-haidt.html.

15. McRaney, D., *The Just-World Fallacy*, Youarenotsosmart.com, 6/07/2010, https://youarenotsosmart.com/2010/06/07/the-just-world-fallacy/.

16. Alicke, M. D., & Govorun, O., *The Better-Than-Average Effect*, The Self in Social Judgment (pp. 85–106). Psychology Press, 2005, https://psycnet.apa.org/record/2005-14648-005.

17. West, K., Eaton, A., *Prejudiced and unaware of it: Evidence for the Dunning-Kruger model in the domains of racism and sexism*, Personality and Individual Differences, Volume 146, Pages 111-119, 8/1/2019, https://www.sciencedirect.com/science/article/abs/pii/S0191886919302156?via%3Dihub.

18. Cross, R., Oakes, K., et al, *Cultivating an Inclusive Culture Through Personal Networks*, MIT Sloan Management Review, 6/08/2021, https://sloanreview.mit.edu/article/cultivating-an-inclusive-culture-through-personal-networks/.

19. Ibid.

20. Kirkland, R., Bohnet, I., *Focusing on what works for workplace diversity*, McKinsey & Co., 4/7/2017, https://www.mckinsey.com/featured-insights/gender-equality/focusing-on-what-works-for-workplace-diversity.

21. Dobbin, F., Kalev, A., *Why Diversity Programs Fail*, Harvard Business Review, July 2016, https://hbr.org/2016/07/why-diversity-programs-fail.

22. Cronbach, L. J., Meehl, P. E., *Construct validity in psychological tests*, Psychological Bulletin, 52(4), 281–302, 1955, https://doi.org/10.1037/h0040957.

23. Dovidio, J., Kawakami, K., *Implicit and explicit prejudice and interracial interaction*, J Pers Soc Psychol, 82(1):62-8, January 2002, https://pubmed.ncbi.nlm.nih.gov/11811635/.

24. Grose, J., *Goodbye to the 'Office Mom'*, New York Times, 9/03/2021, https://www.nytimes.com/2021/09/03/business/goodbye-office-mom.html.

25. Olivet Nazarene University, *RESEARCH ON FRIENDS AT WORK*, 2018, https://online.olivet.edu/news/research-friends-work.

26. Mauss, I. B., Savino, et al, *The pursuit of happiness can be lonely.* Emotion, 12(5), 908–912, 2012, https://doi.org/10.1037/a0025299.

27. Mauss, I. B., Tamir, M., et al, *Can seeking happiness make people unhappy? Paradoxical effects of valuing happiness.* Emotion, 11(4), 807–815, 2011, https://doi.org/10.1037/a0022010.

28. Statista, *Percentage of adults in the U.S. who experienced stress in select situations and areas of their life as of February 2017*, Accessed 2/03/2022, https://www.statista.com/statistics/675233/situations-and-areas-of-life-where-adults-felt-stressed-us/.

29. Loprinzi, P., Branscum, A., *Mayo Clinic Proceedings*, Volume 91, Issue 4, p. 432-442, 4/1/2016, https://www.mayoclinicproceedings.org/article/S0025-6196(16)00043-4/fulltext.

30. American Psychological Association, *Stress in America™: January 2021 Stress Snapshot*, 2/2/2021, https://www.apa.org/news/press/releases/2021/02/adults-stress-pandemic.

31. Geewax, M., *Most Americans Are No Longer Middle Class*, NPR.org, 12/10/2015, https://livingwage.mit.edu/articles/13-the-tipping-point-most-americans-no-longer-are-middle-class.

32. Stover, D., Wood, J., *Most Company Wellness Programs Are a Bust*, Gallup, 2/04/15, https://www.gallup.com/workplace/236516/company-wellness-programs-bust.aspx.

33. Baker, M., Zuech, T., *Gartner HR Research Reveals More Than Half of Employees have Experienced Significant Damage to Their Workforce Health Since the Start of the COVID-19 Pandemic*, Gartner, 6/09/2021, https://www.gartner.com/en/newsroom/press-releases/2021-07-09-gartner-hr-research-

reveals-more-than-half-of-employees-have-experienced-significant-damage-to-their-workforce-health-since-the-start-of-the-covid-19-pandemic.

34. Preidt, R., *Pandemic Tougher on Mental Health For Women Than Men*, Webmd.com, 12/30/2020, https://www.webmd.com/lung/news/20201230/pandemic-may-be-tougher-on-womens-mental-health-than-mens.

35. Galofaro, C., *In pandemic, drug overdose deaths soar among Black Americans*, AP, 6/24/2021, https://apnews.com/article/coronavirus-pandemic-lifestyle-george-floyd-pandemics-health-ea94f4021018bfc7bc88e7b494c8665e.

36. Bosman, J., Kosacove, S., et al, *U.S. Life Expectancy Plunged in 2020, Especially for Black and Hispanic Americans*, New York Times, 7/21/2021, https://www.nytimes.com/2021/07/21/us/american-life-expectancy-report.html.

37. Louis, K., Kufeld, M., et al, *Learning during COVID-19: Reading and math achievement in the 2020-21 school year*, Center for School and Student Progress, Nwea.org, July 2021, https://www.nwea.org/content/uploads/2021/07/Learning-during-COVID-19-Reading-and-math-achievement-in-the-2020-2021-school-year.research-brief-1.pdf.

38. Dorn, E., Hancock, B., et al, *COVID-19 and education: The lingering effects of unfinished learning*, McKinsey & Co., 7/27/2021, https://www.mckinsey.com/industries/education/our-insights/covid-19-and-education-the-lingering-effects-of-unfinished-learning.

39. Hancock, B., Shaninger, B., *The elusive inclusive workplace*, McKinsey & Co., 3/23/2021, https://www.mckinsey.com/business-functions/people-and-organizational-performance/our-insights/the-elusive-inclusive-workplace?cid=other-eml-alt-mip-mck&hdpid=8424a0d5-44a7-42b9-80db-0b9c96c58f86&hctky=10141067&hlkid=9e1aef9614b34e92a4339f422ffe73be.

40. Autin, K., Alan, B., *Socioeconomic Privilege and Meaningful Work: A Psychology of Working Perspective*, Journal of Career Assessment, 6/12/2019, https://journals.sagepub.com/doi/abs/10.1177/1069072719856307.

41. Qualtrics, *2022 Employee Experience Trends Report*, Qualtrics.com, 2022, https://www.qualtrics.com/ebooks-guides/employee-experience-trends-2022/.

42. Stretcher, V., Bremen, J., *Dignity and Purpose in a Pandemic*, Kumanu, Harris Poll, Willis Towers, Watson, Accessed 2/03/2021, https://www.kumanu.com/dignity-and-purpose-in-a-pandemic/.

43. LinkedIn, Imperative, *Purpose at Work 2016 Global Report*, 2016, Imperative, 2016, https://cdn.imperative.com/media/public/Global_Purpose_Index_2016.pdf.

44. BetterUp, *Latest Research on Meaning and Purpose At Work*, 2019, https://grow.betterup.com/resources/meaning-and-purpose-report.

45. DiLeonardo, A., Phelps, R., et al, *Establish a performance culture as your "secret sauce"*, McKinsey & Co., 7/27/2020, https://www.mckinsey.com/business-functions/people-and-organizational-performance/our-insights/the-organization-blog/establish-a-performance-culture-as-your-secret-sauce.

46. Ford, B., Dmitrieva, J., et al, *Culture shapes whether the pursuit of happiness predicts higher or lower well-being*. Journal of Experimental Psychology: General, 144(6), 1053–1062, 2015, https://doi.org/10.1037/xge0000108.

47. Peele, B., Asbaty, C., *The Impact of Small Group Discussions on Behavior Change, Retention and Trust in Large Enterprises*, ion Learning, 10/01/2020, https://www.ionlearning.com/latest/smallgroupstudy.

48. Nagoski, E., Nagoski, A., *Burnout*, Ballantine Books, 2019, https://www.penguinrandomhouse.com/books/592377/burnout-by-emily-nagoski-phd-and-amelia-nagoski-dma/.

49. Levi-Belz, Y., *Growing together: interpersonal predictors of posttraumatic growth trajectory among suicide-loss survivors*, Society, Stress, & Coping, 7/27/2021, https://www.tandfonline.com/doi/abs/10.1080/10615806.2021.1958791.

50. Stretcher, V., Bremen, J., *Dignity and Purpose in a Pandemic*, Kumanu, Harris Poll, Willis Towers, Watson, Accessed 2/03/2021, https://www.kumanu.com/dignity-and-purpose-in-a-pandemic/.

51. Kim, E., Strecher, V., et al, *Purpose and health care use,* Proceedings of the National Academy of Sciences, 111 (46) 16331-16336, November 2014, https://www.pnas.org/content/early/2014/10/29/1414826111.

52. Calmasini C., Swinnerton K., et al, *Association of Social Integration with Cognitive Status in a Multi-Ethnic Cohort: Results From the Kaiser Healthy Aging and Diverse Life Experiences Study*, Journal of Geriatric Psychiatry and Neurology, January 2022, https://pubmed.ncbi.nlm.nih.gov/35077251/.

53. Trudel-Fitzgerald C., Zevon E., et al, *The Prospective Association of Social Integration With Life Span and Exceptional Longevity in Women*, J Gerontol B Psychol Sci Soc Sci. 11/13/2020, https://pubmed.ncbi.nlm.nih.gov/31495897/.

54. Holt-Lunstad J., Smith T., et al, *Social Relationships and Mortality Risk: A Meta-analytic Review.* PLoS Med 7(7): e1000316, 2010 https://doi.org/10.1371/journal.pmed.1000316

55. Sone, T., Nakaya, N. et al, *Sense of Life Worth Living (Ikigai) and Mortality in Japan: Ohsaki Study*, Psychosomatic Medicine: Volume 70 - Issue 6 - p 709-715, July, 2008, https://pubmed.ncbi.nlm.nih.gov/18596247/.

Chapter 5

1. Edelman, *Edelman Trust Barometer 2021*, Edelman.com, 2021, https://www.edelman.com/sites/g/files/aatuss191/files/2021-08/2021EdelmanTrustBarometerSpecialReport_TheBelief-DrivenEmployee.pdf.

2. Baker, M. Zuech, ,T, *Gartner HR Research Reveals More Than Half of Employees have Experienced Significant Damage to Their Workforce Health Since the Start of the COVID-19 Pandemic*, Gartner, 6/09/2021, https://www.gartner.com/en/newsroom/press-releases/2021-07-09-gartner-hr-research-reveals-more-than-half-of-employees-have-experienced-significant-damage-to-their-workforce-health-since-the-start-of-the-covid-19-pandemic.

3. Peele, B., Asbaty, C., *The Impact of Small Group Discussions on Behavior Change, Retention and Trust in Large Enterprises*, ion Learning, 10/01/2020, https://www.ionlearning.com/latest/smallgroupstudy.

4. Hurst, A., *30,000 Conversations: Hybrid Work Research Briefing*, Imperative, 9/14/2021, https://us02web.zoom.us/webinar/register/rec/WN_8lHOIkBZSNWtTHPWDhYFXg?meetingId=IXbko4aQhdewDbz0DQumzbxAdixMvijMw8H3t0hlP3rcrWQ7jur7vQ_eMMuAkbY2.kgY1qlFy_PePCWQS&playId=&action=play&_x_zm_rtaid=sZgCrmzjTIu_dRo6CEoU5g.1644083462826.82b86ee18f44f2926f7f0e5eaf98b9cf&_x_zm_rhtaid=412.

5. Burrow, A., Stanley, M., et al, *Purpose in Life as a Resource for Increasing Comfort With Ethnic Diversity*, Personality and Social Psychology Bulletin, 40(11):1507-1516, 2014, https://journals.sagepub.com/doi/abs/10.1177/0146167214549540.

6. Burrow, A., Hill, P, *Derailed by Diversity? Purpose Buffers the Relationship Between Ethnic Composition on Trains and Passenger Negative Mood*, Personality and Social Psychology Bulletin, 39(12):1610-1619, 2013, https://journals.sagepub.com/doi/abs/10.1177/0146167213499377.

7. Mariano, J., Damiani, T., et al, *Self- and Other-Reported Virtues of Young Purpose Exemplars*, Youth & Society, 53(3):466-485, 2021,https://journals.sagepub.com/doi/abs/10.1177/0044118X19859022.

8. Malin, H., Liaow, I., et al, *Purpose and Character Development in Early Adolescence*, J Youth Adolescence 46:1200–1215, 2017, https://ggsc.berkeley.edu/images/uploads/Malin_et_al_Purpose_and_Character_Development_in_Early_Adolescence.pdf

9. Crocker, J., Niiya, Y., et al, *Why does writing about important values reduce defensiveness? Self-affirmation and the role of positive other-directed feelings*, Psychol Sci, (7):740-7, 7/19/2008, https://pubmed.ncbi.nlm.nih.gov/18727791/;

10. Gallup / Healthways, *State of Global Wellbeing*, 2013, Healthways.com, http://info.healthways.com/hs-fs/hub/162029/file-1634508606-pdf/WBI2013/Gallup-Healthways_State_of_Global_Well-Being_vFINAL.pdf?t=1428689269171.

11. Baumeister, R., Vohs, K., et al, *Some key differences between a happy life and a meaningful life*, The Journal of Positive Psychology, 8:6, 505-516, 2013,https://www.semanticscholar.org/paper/Some-key-differences-between-a-happy-life-and-a-Baumeister-Vohs/559085745da7b6b58e560c6c671c7ac7fafe8a97.

12. Hancock, B., Shaninger, B., *The elusive inclusive workplace*, McKinsey & Co., 3/23/2021, https://www.mckinsey.com/business-functions/people-and-organizational-performance/our-insights/the-elusive-inclusive-workplace?cid=other-eml-alt-mip-mck&hdpid=8424a0d5-44a7-42b9-80db-0b9c96c58f86&hctky=10141067&hlkid=9e1aef9614b34e92a4339f422ffe73be.

13. Madrazo, V., *Identity, Purpose, and Well-Being Among Emerging Adult Hispanic Women*, 7/02/2014, Florida International University, https://digitalcommons.fiu.edu/cgi/viewcontent.cgi?referer=&httpsredir=1&article=2698&context=etd.

14. Rainey, L., *The Search for Purpose in Life: An Exploration of Purpose, the Search Process, and Purpose Anxiety*, University of Pennsylvania, August 2014, https://repository.upenn.edu/cgi/viewcontent.cgi?referer=&httpsredir=1&article=1061&context=mapp_capstone.

15. Hurst, A., *2019 Workforce Purpose Index*, Imperative, 2019, https://www.imperative.com/2019wpi.

16. Purdue Global, *Generational Differences in the Workplace*, 2021, https://www.purdueglobal.edu/education-partnerships/generational-workforce-differences-infographic/.

17. BetterUp, *Latest Research on Meaning and Purpose At Work*, Betterup, 2019, https://grow.betterup.com/resources/meaning-and-purpose-report.

18. Dingra, N., Samo, A., et al, *Help your employees find purpose—or watch them leave*, McKinsey & Co. 4/5/2021, https://www.mckinsey.com/business-functions/people-and-organizational-performance/our-insights/help-your-employees-find-purpose-or-watch-them-leave.

19. Google Trends, *"purpose in life"*, accessed May 2019, https://trends.google.com/trends/.

20. BetterUp, *Latest Research on Meaning and Purpose At Work*, BetterUp, 2019, https://grow.betterup.com/resources/meaning-and-purpose-report.

21. Dingra, N., Samo, A., et al, *Help your employees find purpose—or watch them leave*, McKinsey & Co. 4/5/2021, https://www.mckinsey.com/business-functions/people-and-organizational-performance/our-insights/help-your-employees-find-purpose-or-watch-them-leave.

22. Cone / Porter Novelli, *Purpose Study*, Conecomm.com, 2018, https://www.conecomm.com/research-blog/2018-purpose-study#download-the-research.

23. Edelman, *2017 Trust Barometer*, 2017, https://www.edelman.com/trust/2017-trust-barometer.

24. Edelman, *Edelman Trust Barometer 2021*, 2021, https://www.edelman.com/sites/g/files/aatuss191/files/2021-08/2021EdelmanTrustBarometerSpecialReport_TheBelief-DrivenEmployee.pdf.

25. Ibid.

26. Kohlman, S., *The Ships Are Burning: A No-BS Guide to Organizational Culture, Trust and Workplace Meaning*, Gatekeeper Press, 2020, https://smile.amazon.com/Ships-Are-Burning-Organizational-Workplace-ebook/dp/B08HJ7CW6Q.

27. Coqual, *The Power of Belonging*, 2020, https://coqual.org/wp-content/uploads/2020/09/CoqualPowerOfBelongingKeyFindings090720.pdf.

28. BetterUp, T*he Value of Belonging at Work: New Frontiers for Inclusion in 2021 and Beyond*, 2021, https://grow.betterup.com/resources/the-value-of-belonging-at-work-the-business-case-for-investing-in-workplace-inclusion.

29. Hurst, A., *2019 Workforce Purpose Index*, Imperative, 2019, https://www.imperative.com/2019wpi.

30. Peele, B., Asbaty, C., *The Impact of Small Group Discussions on Behavior Change, Retention and Trust in Large Enterprises*, ion Learning, 10/01/2020, https://www.ionlearning.com/latest/smallgroupstudy.

31. Centola, D., *Change*, Little, Brown, Spark, 2021, https://www.amazon.com/dp/B0859TZWVG/ref=dp-kindle-redirect?_encoding=UTF8&btkr=1.

32. Dingra, N., Samo, A., et al, *Help your employees find purpose—or watch them leave*, McKinsey & Co. 4/5/2021, https://www.mckinsey.com/business-functions/people-and-organizational-performance/our-insights/help-your-employees-find-purpose-or-watch-them-leave.

33. Cross, R., Oakes, K., et al, *Cultivating an Inclusive Culture Through Personal Networks*, MIT Sloan Management Review, 6/08/2021, https://sloanreview.mit.edu/article/cultivating-an-inclusive-culture-through-personal-networks/.

34. Burt, R., *Structural Holes: The Social Structure of Competition*, University of Illinois at Urbana-Champaign's Academy for Entrepreneurial Leadership Historical Research Reference in Entrepreneurship, 1992, https://ssrn.com/abstract=1496205.

35. Cross, R., Oakes, K., et al, *Cultivating an Inclusive Culture Through Personal Networks*, MIT Sloan Management Review, 6/08/2021, https://sloanreview.mit.edu/article/cultivating-an-inclusive-culture-through-personal-networks/.

36. Phillips, K., *How Diversity Makes Us Smarter*, Scientific American, October 2014, https://www.scientificamerican.com/article/how-diversity-makes-us-smarter/.

37. Ford, B., Dmitrieva, J., et al,*Culture shapes whether the pursuit of happiness predicts higher or lower well-being*, Journal of Experimental Psychology: General, 144(6), 1053–1062, 2015, https://doi.org/10.1037/xge0000108.

38. Trudel-Fitzgerald C., Zevon E., et al, *The Prospective Association of Social Integration With Life Span and Exceptional Longevity in Women*, J Gerontol B Psychol Sci Soc Sci, 75(10):2132-2141, 11/13/2020, https://pubmed.ncbi.nlm.nih.gov/31495897/.

39. Rath, T., Harter, J., *Wellbeing*, Gallup Press, 2010, https://smile.amazon.com/dp/B01A67ID8M/ref=dp-kindle-redirect?_encoding=UTF8&btkr=1.

40. Nagoski, E., Nagoski, A., *Burnout*, Ballantine Books, 2019, https://www.penguinrandomhouse.com/books/592377/burnout-by-emily-nagoski-phd-and-amelia-nagoski-dma/.

41. McMahon, N., Visram, S. et al, *Mechanisms of change of a novel weight loss programme provided by a third sector organisation: a qualitative interview study*, BMC Public Health, 16, 378, 2016, https://doi.org/10.1186/s12889-016-3063-4.

42. Cruwys, T., Haslam, S., et al, *"That's not what we do": Evidence that normative change is a mechanism of action in group interventions"*, Behaviour Research and Therapy, Volume 65, Pages 11-17, February 2015, https://www.sciencedirect.com/science/article/abs/pii/S000579671400196X?via%3Dihub.

43. Sani, F., Madhok, V., et al, *Greater number of group identifications is associated with healthier behaviour: Evidence from a Scottish community sample*, British Journal of Health Psychology, Volume20, Issue3, Pages 466-481, September 2015, https://bpspsychub.onlinelibrary.wiley.com/doi/abs/10.1111/bjhp.12119.

44. Haslam, C., Cruwys, T., et al, *Evidence that a social-identity intervention that builds and strengthens social group membership improves mental health*, Journal of Affective Disorders, Volume 194, Pages 188-195, April 2016, https://www.sciencedirect.com/science/article/abs/pii/S0165032715312180?via%3Dihub.

45. Smith-Turchyn, J., Morgan, A., et al, *The Effectiveness of Group-based Self-management Programmes to Improve Physical and Psychological Outcomes in Patients with Cancer: a Systematic Review and Meta-analysis of Randomised Controlled Trials*, Clinical Oncology, VOLUME 28, ISSUE 5, P292-305, 5/1/2016, https://www.clinicaloncologyonline.net/article/S0936-6555(15)00389-1/fulltext.

46. Craig, N., Snook, S., *From Purpose to Impact*, Harvard Business Review, May 2014, https://hbr.org/2014/05/from-purpose-to-impact.

47. Burlingame, G., Fuhriman, A., et al, *The differential effectiveness of group psychotherapy: A meta-analytic perspective*, Group Dynamics: Theory, Research, and Practice, 7(1), 3–12, 2013, https://doi.org/10.1037/1089-2699.7.1.3.

48. Haidt, J., *The emotional dog and its rational tail: A social intuitionist approach to moral judgment*, Psychological Review, 108(4), 814–834, 2001, https://doi.org/10.1037/0033-295X.108.4.814.

49. Zhang, Y., Zhao, R., et al, *Enhancing virtual team performance via high-quality interpersonal relationships: effects of authentic leadership*, International Journal of Manpower, 2021, https://doi.org/10.1108/IJM-08-2020-0378.

50. Soboroff, S., *Group size and the trust, cohesion, and commitment of group members*, University of Iowa, Autumn 2012, https://citeseerx.ist.psu.edu/viewdoc/download?doi=10.1.1.452.6454&rep=rep1&type=pdf.

51. Tang, L., *Perceived Power Hierarchy and Psychological Safety on Team Effectiveness*, Deloitte, 10/22/2019, https://www2.deloitte.com/au/en/blog/diversity-inclusion-blog/2019/perceived-power-hierarchy-psychological-safety-on-team-effectiveness.html.

52. Zhan, Z., Fong, P., et al, *Effects of gender grouping on students' group performance, individual achievements and attitudes in computer-supported collaborative learning*, Computers in Human Behavior, 48. 587-596, 2015, https://www.researchgate.net/publication/276835655_Effects_of_gender_grouping_on_students%27_group_performance_individual_achievements_and_attitudes_in_computer-supported_collaborative_learning.

53. Watson, W., Johnson, L., et al, *The influence of ethnic diversity on leadership, group process, and performance: an examination of learning teams*, International Journal of Intercultural Relations, Volume 26, Issue 1, Pages 1-16, 2002, https://doi.org/10.1016/S0147-1767(01)00032-3.

54. DeAngelis, T, *All you need is contact*, Monitor on Psychology, 32(10), November, 2001, http://www.apa.org/monitor/nov01/contact.

55. Pettigrew, T., Tropp, L., *A meta-analytic test of intergroup contact theory*, Journal of Personality and Social Psychology, 90(5), 751–783, 2006, https://doi.org/10.1037/0022-3514.90.5.751.

56. Cross, R., Tina, R., et al, *Connect and adapt: How network development and transformation improve retention and engagement in employees' first five years*, Organizational Dynamics, 2017, https://www.semanticscholar.org/paper/Connect-and-adapt%3A-How-network-development-and-and-Cross-Opie/e2d2fd1a8645031db2a065cec6e6f3c7cf82d282.

57. Yang, L., Holtz, D., et al, *The effects of remote work on collaboration among information workers*, Nat Hum Behav 6, 43–54, 2022, https://doi.org/10.1038/s41562-021-01196-4

58. Murre, J. M., Dros, J, *Replication and Analysis of Ebbinghaus' Forgetting Curve*, PloS one, 10(7), e0120644, 2015, https://doi.org/10.1371/journal.pone.0120644.

59. Hurst, A., *30,000 Conversations: Hybrid Work Research Briefing*, Imperative, 9/14/2021, https://us02web.zoom.us/webinar/register/rec/WN_8lHOIkBZSNWtTHPWDhYFXg?meetingId=IXbko4aQhdewDbz0DQumzbxAdixMvijMw8H3t0hlP3rcrWQ7jur7vQ_eMMuAkbY2.kgY1qlFy_PeP

CWQS&playId=&action=play&_x_zm_rtaid=sZgCrmzjTIu_dRo6CEoU5g.1644083462826.82b86e
e18f44f2926f7f0e5eaf98b9cf&_x_zm_rhtaid=412.
60. Peele, B., Asbaty, C., *The Impact of Small Group Discussions on Behavior Change, Retention and Trust in Large Enterprises*, ion Learning, 10/01/2020,
https://www.ionlearning.com/latest/smallgroupstudy.
61. Centola, D., *Change*, Little, Brown, Spark, 2021,
https://www.amazon.com/dp/B0859TZWVG/ref=dp-kindle-redirect?_encoding=UTF8&btkr=1.

Chapter 6

1. Rey, C., Prat, M., et al, *Purpose-driven Organizations Management Ideas for a Better World*: Open Access, 10.1007/978-3-030-17674-7, 2019,
https://www.researchgate.net/publication/333838296_Purpose-driven_Organizations_Management_Ideas_for_a_Better_World_Management_Ideas_for_a_Better_World_Open_Acces.
2. Ibid.
3. BetterUp, *Latest Research on Meaning and Purpose At Work*, 2019,
https://grow.betterup.com/resources/meaning-and-purpose-report.
4. Schwartz, N., *Pay Cuts Become a Tool for Some Companies to Avoid Layoffs*, New York Times, 5/24/2020, https://www.nytimes.com/2020/05/24/business/economy/coronavirus-pay-cuts.html.
5. Centola, D., *Change*, Little, Brown, Spark, 2021,
https://www.amazon.com/dp/B0859TZWVG/ref=dp-kindle-redirect?_encoding=UTF8&btkr=1.
6. Graeber, D., *Bullshit Jobs: A Theory*, Simon & Schuster, 2018,
https://smile.amazon.com/Bullshit-Jobs-Theory-David-Graeber-ebook/dp/B075RWG7YM/ref=sr_1_1?crid=HZOSLVDDTT7Y&keywords=bullshit+jobs&qid=1644512242&s=digital-text&sprefix=bullshit+job%2Cdigital-text%2C166&sr=1-1.
7. McChrystal, S., Collins, T., et al, *Team of Teams: New Rules of Engagement for a Complex World*, Portfolio, 2015, https://smile.amazon.com/Team-Teams-Rules-Engagement-Complex/dp/1591847486.

About the Author

B randon Peele (he/him) is a Midwesterner, best-selling author, the CEO of Unity Lab, and an expert in purpose, leadership + culture change. He's trusted as a keynote speaker, consultant and program leader by organizations such as Google, Johnson & Johnson, Stanford University, JDRF, Morgan Stanley, U.S. Marine Corps, University of California - Berkeley, LinkedIn, the U.S. Navy, Slalom Consulting, the U.S. Coast Guard, and the University of Minnesota.

His previous books include *The Purpose Field Guide* (2019) and *Planet on Purpose* (2018). He is also the co-author of *Purpose Rising* (2017) and *The Purpose Blueprint* (2015) and his work has been featured by news organizations such as USA Today, U.S. News & World Report, and Forbes.

Brandon holds an MBA in Leadership from Columbia Business School, is an Imperative Certified Purpose Leader^{TM}, and serves on the Council of the Global Purpose Leaders and the Leadership Council of ManKind Project San Diego.

Made in the USA
Middletown, DE
26 April 2022

64784436R00111